South Carolina
in 1865

Karen Stokes

Published by The History Press
Charleston, SC
www.historypress.com

Copyright © 2022 by Karen Stokes
All rights reserved

First published 2022

Manufactured in the United States

ISBN 9781467151344

Library of Congress Control Number: 2021949173

Notice: The information in this book is true and complete to the best of our knowledge. It is offered without guarantee on the part of the author or The History Press. The author and The History Press disclaim all liability in connection with the use of this book.

All rights reserved. No part of this book may be reproduced or transmitted in any form whatsoever without prior written permission from the publisher except in the case of brief quotations embodied in critical articles and reviews.

Contents

Acknowledgements 5
Introduction 7

I. Letters North and South
   Josephine LeConte's Harrowing Tale 10
   Private Grundy's Letter 18
   The Middleton Ladies in Columbia 20
   Alfred Huger's Letter 31

II. The Burning of Columbia
   Lieutenant Platter's Diary 38
   William B. Yates's Nightmare 40
   Ilium in Flames 42
   Mrs. Lee's Fiery Ordeal 80
   Edwin J. Scott's Columbia Diary 91

III. 1865 in the Lowcountry
   Contemplating Desolation: Occupied Charleston 104
   The War in Berkeley County: Frederick A. Porcher's Account 119

Epilogue 131
Notes 135
Bibliography 141
About the Author 144

Acknowledgements

As always, I am indebted to the South Carolina Historical Society for the inspiration and materials found in its rich manuscript collections. I am also grateful to Dr. James E. Kibler, who brought several resources to my attention, and to the staffs of the Bancroft Library at the University of California–Berkeley, the University of South Carolina Archives and the Richland Library in Columbia, South Carolina.

Introduction

The American Civil War, which lasted from 1861 to 1865, was not just a conflict fought out on battlefields by opposing armies—it also involved warfare against civilians, which took place almost exclusively in the South. In 1865, this kind of total war against noncombatants and their property was carried out most conspicuously in South Carolina by Union troops under the command of General William T. Sherman. Beginning in early 1865, his massive army of over sixty thousand troops cut a swath of destruction across the state from the coast to the North Carolina border, meeting with little effective military resistance from the much smaller number of Confederate troops present in South Carolina. In March 1865, Sherman's forces moved into North Carolina. The following month, General Robert E. Lee surrendered the Army of Northern Virginia at Appomattox Court House, and General Joseph E. Johnston surrendered his army in North Carolina. Soon afterward, the remaining Confederate forces also surrendered, and the war was over.

The surviving records of this crucial year in the state's history are numerous and revealing and include many eyewitness accounts of South Carolinians who lived through it. What has been called "the most monstrous barbarity of the barbarous march"[1] was the destruction of South Carolina's capital, Columbia—a city full of women, children and old men that had been surrendered by its mayor, only to be sacked and burned by Sherman's soldiers. This book features letters written by Columbia residents in 1865 and some of their later memoirs describing the terrors and trauma of that event.

Mary Maxcy Leverett, the wife of Reverend Charles Edward, an Episcopal minister, watched Columbia burn from her house just outside the city, which was also visited by Sherman's troops. A month later, she wrote to a cousin:

Introduction

You will wish to hear how we fared, & just think for a moment how you would feel, if you suddenly found what seemed to be hundreds of Yankees pouring through your house, breaking open drawers, destroying, stealing everything to eat or to wear, often destroying what they could not, loading our own wagon with it all, making my own servants chop off the heads of about thirty head of ducks, turkeys, fowls & guinea fowls & throw them into the wagon, & I standing in the back piazza silently looking on! [2]

While Columbia burned, the undefended city of Charleston was occupied by Union troops who launched raids into the surrounding countryside, including the rich plantation lands of a neighboring area that is now Berkeley County. In 1868, historian Frederick A. Porcher, a native of that area, wrote about these destructive raids conducted by soldiers under the command of General Alfred S. Hartwell and General E.E. Potter.

Because it was the "cradle of secession," South Carolina was singled out for particularly savage treatment by the Northern army. Sherman's campaign in 1865 wrought extensive destruction and loss, and the state also suffered tremendous losses in men who had gone into military service to fight in the armies of the Confederacy. In 2005, reflecting on the South Carolina's condition after the war, Walter B. Edgar observed:

The war that had begun in Charleston in April 1861 destroyed a South Carolina that had existed for nearly two centuries. From August 1863 until February 1865, Charleston was under continuous bombardment from enemy guns and mortars. Below Calhoun Street, the city was a ghost town. The state's losses, even from the distance of seven-score years, are horrific. Major portions of Columbia, Charleston, and twenty-one villages lay in ruins. With emancipation, more than one half of the total wealth of the state disappeared. In terms of livestock, South Carolina suffered greater losses than any other state. By 1867 land values had declined 60 percent. As staggering as the property losses were, the toll in human lives was even greater. Some 60,000 sons of Carolina entered military service—virtually the entire white male population of military age in 1860. Of these, 21,146 (35 percent) were killed, a percentage twice that of England, France, Germany, and Russia in World War I when Europe "lost" a generation. "The war," wrote John Berkeley Grimball, "has ruined us." The old prewar elite was out of power at all levels of government from 1868 until 1877.

How this world ended is presented in the personal and historical accounts that follow.

I

Letters North and South

Josephine LeConte's Harrowing Tale

Josephine LeConte was the wife of John LeConte, a professor of physics at South Carolina College (now the University of South Carolina). They lived in a fine brick house on the corner of Pendleton and Sumter Streets in Columbia. Built by the college in 1860, it was known as the "Fourth Professor's House." During the night and early morning hours of February 17, Sherman's soldiers made several attempts to burn the LeConte home. John LeConte, a supervisor of the Confederate Nitre and Mining Bureau, had been ordered away, but fortunately, a family friend named Dr. Carter was present that night. With his help, as well as the heroic efforts of the LeConte ladies, the house was preserved from destruction.

In a letter that Josephine LeConte wrote to her son about ten days later, she reported the fate of her husband and his companions and, recalling the horrors of the night of February 17, described how some of Sherman's drunken soldiers were burned to death in a city hospital. Other Union soldiers, finding the corpses and thinking that they were dead Confederates, "severed the heads from the bodies, caught them up on their bayonets, and danced around to the tune of 'damnation to the rebels.'"

The letter is presented as it was originally written, preserving Mrs. LeConte's spelling, punctuation and capitalization.

Columbia, S.C. Feb 28th '65
My own darling Boy—

Oh me! What hours of agony and suspence I have endured since you left me on the morning of the 15th. On the 16th your father left, in company with Capt Green and your Uncle Joe carrying with them a large amount of Baggage. I sent off every stitch of Lula's and my body clothing, all the blankets, towels, table linen sheets and your body, your brothers also, Johnnie Hardens Mitchell, Champions, Sammie Jones, and silver cups—waiters, pitchers, sugar bowls, and some silk dresses of your Aunt Jane's and Ada's, besides all my curtains and numberless other rich [racks] of value. They had not gone over 25 miles when they were overtaken by a party of Morgan's command and turned over to the provost guard of Jeff Davis Corps. Your father and brother were by the waggons keeping watch while your Uncle Joe and Capt Green were out scouting, the alarm being given your uncle and Green had time to escape but your father and brother were taken prisoners. All our effects were then broken open a bonfire made of all our clothing but the valuables were also carried off. Your father had a gun put to his breast and his watch demanded which he gave up at once, but a Capt Craft coming up took the watch from the soldier and put it in his pocket to keep for your father. The next day your brother was paroled, and allowed to come home, he brought with him a good deal of the funds belonging to the Bureau and as he was leaving the camp the officers tossed my velvet cloak to him knowing it had belonged to his family and asked him if he did not wish it. Johnnie eagerly seized it besides some daguerreotypes that belong to Mitchel or Champion.

   Besides the clothes we stand in and a couple of dresses Sandy brought back for Lula are all the clothing we have in this world. The family pictures and mementoes of all sorts besides your father's books and papers and all our letters were destroyed by the burning of Dr O'Connels House. The house that covers us—a limited supply of provisions, and some funds are all that we are now worth—I will not despair if your father only returns and you can whip Sherman. London has returned—Peter and Somer were carried off—Peter told London that he should return, but

Eleanor Josephine LeConte (1824–1894), circa 1850. Her son Louis Julian served in the Chatham Artillery, CSA. *Bancroft Library, University of California–Berkeley.*

Somer was so fascinated by the Gypsy life of the Army that he told London he would not come back again. It seems a Yankee fancied him and stripped a fellow to rig him up, put boots on his feet and gave him a pony and the last seen of him he was flying around in grand style.

Keep a sharp look out for Morgan's command—Jeff Davis Corps—for I feel if Peter can't get away any other way and opposing forces meet you will be sure to meet him. They try to console me that your father will soon be paroled but I have my doubts—They labored so faithfully to get your uncle and Capt Green and at times their escape was so miraculous that I fear they will visit their chagrin on him. Johnnie says they were kind to them (Dr Wallace of Columbia was caught at the same time) and treated them with every courtesy. Johnnie was as saucy as possible to them and used to answer them back on all occasions—very much to their amusement. They all called your father major from the start, seemed posted on all points which I can't help thinking very strange. One of them said to Johnnie—"The first thing you must learn to do my boy is steal." "Thank you said Johnnie none of you had to learn that for it comes very natural to you." Then the

Yanks would roar with laughter and begin again at him—from his account he handled them with his gloves off.

I shall leave your father and turn now the events more closely at home—As Johnnie Harden left our door the Yanks were coming up Main Street. He could not have gone far before the stars and stripes were floating on the old State House—in a few seconds more the same thing happened to the new but what delighted my eyes was to see their battle flag blown right in two as they attempted to raise it. The wind springing up at the same time prevented their flaunting them in our faces. With effect—the whole of Logan's Corps 25 thousand men passed by our door about [4 o'clock] with their various bands of music and flags. I hardly ever saw a more hardy vigorous set of men, well clothed and fine equipments in all respects. About six in the evening their work of destruction began, the city was fired simultaneously from all points and certainly a night of more awful horrors I never passed or conceived of. About 5 in the afternoon young Sergeant Trumbo stopped before our gate [and] he comforted me by telling you were still safe but that the fighting was going on and when he left shortly after Dr Carter called to give us some encouragement. We prevailed upon him to remain which he did—from that time untill he left for his native city Augusta he proved himself a most devoted friend. Nothing could surpass his generous self sacrificing care for us and to him we owe our preservation. The picture of misery and woe of our beloved city is indescribable. Nothing remains intact but the Campus grounds, Theological Seminary—the new State House, which they hadn't the powder to blow up—female college—and the Catholic church, our Episcopal church (Christ Church was burnt) the baptist, methodist and presbyterian churches—all more or less damaged and every effort made to burn them failed thro the exertions of their friends. One or two rows of buildings skirting the town are all that are left by that Vandal horde. For a long time we were in imminent danger from the flames all around us as the Piazza caught, but Dr Carter was faithful, in watching the embers and extinguishing them as they caught. To show you what villains those Yankees were they screamed out to him from the street what was he putting out the fire for? Now recollect this was from the guard that was stationed around the house to protect it. About 11 o'cl[ock] at night, there was a brigade sent to the

South Carolina in 1865

The 13th Iowa raising the Union Flag on the new (unfinished) State Capitol at Columbia, South Carolina.

Sherman's troops raised the United States flag over the new South Carolina statehouse under construction on February 17, 1865. *Wikimedia Commons.*

campus to protect it. Shortly after a furious knocking at the front door tempted me to go and open. As we ladies did so, a fellow flushed with wine and every other evil passion stamped upon his face sprang in and would have immediately commenced pillage but for the ubiquitous Carter who demanded his business in such an authoritative manner that the fellow abashed at seeing a man where he only expected a number of lonely women—turned upon his heel and pretended he only came to give assistance. Carter at once ordered him to furnish it which he acquiesced in after a while by sending <u>two</u> men....

The night seemed endless as we struggled against the fiery embers, while on the street below a throng of vengeful bluecoats appeared to rejoice in the travail. As each house was enveloped in flames their demoniac yells of delight coupled with the shrieks and screams of widdows and orphans who sought the lawn for asylum in front of our house for protection beggars description.

All night long from the Piazza and roof the women fought the flames and there were times when the panes of glass were so hot that you could not rest your hand there for any time but still we fought—and there stood that sea of upturned faces of Logan's Corps with not one spark of sympathy for us. There was no light or water on the campus for the first thing these devils did was to blow up the gas and destroy the waterworks—we were absolutely in their power and bitterly did we grieve over it. At daylight the flames began to subside and I threw myself upon the bed to rest when tramp, tramp, tramp, resounded through the house, upon rising, found that half doz[en] fellows had entered the house from the Kitchen declaring the house was on fire rushed up to the garret pretending to put out the fire—when lo and behold they tore up the tin and deliberately set my house afire.

As the main army was about moving off they sent the provost guard to encamped just in front of my house. The officer in command Major Seay of Iowa and staff—rode up to our front gate to know if they could obtain quarters. Dr Carter suggested it would secure further molestation if we took some of them in. I cannot say they were gentlemen but they certainly treated us with every courtesy by not intruding upon our privacy. We were

The LeConte home, circa 1900. It was later relocated on campus and is now known as Flinn Hall. *Courtesy of University of South Carolina Archives.*

in great terror lest when the main army disappeared we should be burnt out by the stragglers who had vowed vengeance against our house and the college buildings. Our house they seemed to have a particular spite against us for no other reason that I can now see but that we kept so within doors and with every door and blind shut tight—they thought this defiant and of course were itching to get at the inside of it. They took nothing from your father's library nor disturbed the books if I except the bottle of ink. They however left their names and command written upon the wall in a conspicuous place <u>there</u> they <u>shall</u> <u>remain</u> as long as I live here.

About 11 on Sunday morning after that awful night they brought all the combustible materials for burning the college but by the prompt measures of Dr Thompson who denounced them and the active measures of the commanding Generals the buildings were saved, not however before some of the torch bearers tasted of cold steel. I am sure it was the presence of <u>their</u> own men in our Hospital that saved it nothing else.

They burned the Ladies Hospital—fortunately all the sick were removed to our [campus] Hospital during the day except the corpse of one man. During the carnival of death and destruction a number of their own men sought a bed there as their beastly intoxication could carry them no farther—these were burned up—As the flames progressed they could be seen tearing their hair and screaming for help—but help there was none—and when the building fell in they all perished. Instantly the yells of delight filled the air, frantically they advanced, severed the heads from the bodies, caught them up on their bayonets, and danced around to the tune of "damnation to the rebels" little dreaming that they were their own men. Our ladies were insulted on all sides by vile language, but I have not heard of any violations—the negro element surpassed itself for outlawry, billets of burning wood would be thrown at their heads and every species of insulting language use to their owners—immense droves of them left with army—many families were left without one, and all now doing all their work—Annie and Bobbie remained faithful among the faithless in fact she has helped to feed us from the plunder acquired when the stores were thrown open. Bessie's all intended to leave, but finding the army could not furnish waggons for them to ride in concluded to remain. [Mag] and Adams were burnt out—they also left with army besides thousands of other white people. You wonder as you pick your way through the ruins what has become of the people and where have they gone to? You can walk miles about our city and never meet a soul the sense of loneliness and desolation is intolerable. I am about writing to all my friends for help in the way of food. I have enough for present purposes but we must look ahead—fortunately we have funds enough on hand to help us along for some time. If your father were only back I should cease to grieve....Your uncle Joseph is home and will shortly go down to the Manning settlement for supplies, after that they propose going to Augusta that is Capt Green and himself—to procure some clothing. Capt Green and his wife are staying with us it adds to my cares but security also.

The Gibbes were burnt out—didn't save a second stitch of clothing, this is the fate of <u>all</u> our friends. Do let us hear from you every opportunity that offers no matter how few the lines they will be a comfort to my heart. God bless you! My own precious boy and when the opportunity offers strike a blow that that accursed race shall feel in defense for your desolated home and unhappy mother.

Private Grundy's Letter

P rivate Charles Grundy served in General Sherman's army with Company B of the Tenth Illinois Infantry Regiment. Census records indicate that he was born in England in 1839 and immigrated to the United States in 1851. He enlisted in August 1861 and was mustered out of service on July 4, 1865. After General Lee's surrender at Appomattox Court House in Virginia on April 9, 1865, General Joseph E. Johnston surrendered the Confederate troops under his command to General Sherman later that month in North Carolina. In this letter written from Raleigh, Private Grundy expresses his contempt for the enemy and confides to his friend Henry that his army had committed atrocities during the Carolinas campaign that "would have shocked a demon."

Camp near Raleigh, N.C. April 26th, 1865
Dear Friend Henry,

It's a long long time since I last heard from you, and I guess it is a still greater period since you heard from me....I would like to tell you about our Campaign through all of S.C. and a portion of N.C....Some things I saw done on that Campaign would have shocked a demon, and what more the world will remain in ignorance of it, save such as the most important events, but the horrors, atrocities & crimes, I guess they will never be known save as the soldiers relate them to their friends.

Of the Burning of Columbia the proud capitol of the Palmetto State, that occurred on the night of February 17 and of all nights that I may live through hereafter, or may have lived through in the past, I shall ever remember the night at Edisto and that at Columbia. I never could describe the scenes on that night of the conflagration, the shrieking and weeping of women and wringing of hands, the crackling of the flames which tore mercilessly through the doomed city sparing neither the abode of the poor or the magnificent dwellings of the rich, of the shouts and yells of the drunken soldiers, and the indiscriminate plundering and pillaging of houses and stores....It beat anything I ever saw since the War began. I saw it. I was in town all night until daylight in the morn. Just imagine a city of 16000 inhabitants on fire and the populance turned out of doors with just such baggage as they could carry off with them. I guess the entire city save a few houses in the suburbs was destroyed. But it was South Carolina and as the boys said, they took particular pains to "Give her Hell" and I am inclined that a good portion of the time, during Sherman's raid, he was nearly as warm as the climate of that famous place is reported to be...

The Middleton Ladies in Columbia

During the war, many residents of the South Carolina Lowcountry left the coastal area to take refuge in places where they believed they would be safe from the enemy. The wife and daughters of Henry Augustus Middleton, a wealthy rice planter of Georgetown District, spent a couple of years in Flat Rock, North Carolina, before deciding to move to Columbia in 1864. About a week after the burning of the city, one of the daughters, Harriott Middleton, wrote a letter to her cousin Susan M. Middleton describing the family's terrifying experiences. As the Middleton ladies watched houses burning all around their neighborhood, their terror was intensified when a Northern soldier acting as their guard warned them that it was his army's intention to leave "not one house" standing in Columbia. "Do you not see there are no guards in the streets, the city is given up to the soldiery?" he told them. "Go with your things into the garden if the house catches. I will stay with you and guard you as long as I can, but I must soon leave you to your fate."

Columbia, Tuesday 28th
My dearest Susan,

I do not know whether this letter will ever reach you, but I must make an effort to tell you of your belongings in this part of the world. Your house has not suffered much. Isabella went to see after it the afternoon of the day the Yankees left, and I will tell you what I think Nelly told her, but I will pretend to no accuracy, as minds are so perturbed that I neither hear distinctly nor remember accurately, and say what I do not mean by accident.[3]

Nelly carried your father's portrait to the asylum and it was saved. Ella's was carried off.[4] Isa understood Nelly to say that your mother had carried off hers with her. The china clock, and I think she said some few other things were smashed. A box of mine upstairs and one which was buried were seized upon. Some officers had been in the house and it presented a most dirty forlorn appearance when Isabella saw it. Nelly says they were very rude and insulting and threatened to drink up Mr. Oliver's heart blood!! That he was a terrible old rebel, etc![5] Nelly said what I think must be mistake, that the letters about Oliver had been left, and the Yankees took them & read them all, and I understood her to say either carried off or destroyed them. I hope that this may prove to be a mistake.

Mary has lost almost everything. All her silver except two or three pieces was carried off. I understand (don't vouch for the truth) that they put her carpets and other things in the middle of one of the rooms, set fire to them and burned them up, smashed the china and furniture and carried off or destroyed the provisions. The main part if that is correct as I had it both from Nelly and Miss Parker, who told me that after the Yankees left, her Mother went over to save what she could, but only found a few trifles. All their furniture in the house was destroyed. About the plantation—Hal told me yesterday she had seen Bella who told her that only three of the young men had gone off.[6] The enemy drove off the cattle, destroyed the looms, but left the food, only telling the negroes that they were masters of everything.

Among the servants in town only a son of Bella's went off and when ten miles out of town they put him out of the wagon in the road and he came back minus all of his goods in a very penitent frame of mind. So you see you have not suffered very much, and I am as thankful that your Mother was not here. She would have suffered so much tho' all of you would doubtless have behaved like heroines!

Your man Henry brought Hal your letter safely. He was very much ill-treated by the Yankee army. They stole his coat, money and knife and beat him severely. He passed them this side of Winnsboro.

Raven Lewis has died of the Yankees.[7] She was in a very agitated state all the time they were here. It brought on a premature confinement and she and her baby left this world of trouble within forty-eight hours. If her excitement could have been lessened, if she could only have slept, her life would have been saved, but nothing could bring her rest. The whole time the Yankees were here she was in fear and trembling. Her baby is believed to have been accidentally strangled. Though only a seven months' child it was doing well and shortly before the Mother died was sleeping sweetly. Half an hour after her death the nurse brought it into Cousin Caroline black in the face and neck. She and the Doctor say that it was certainly strangled, probably by being put on its back which is said always to suffocate newborn babies, and the nurse never would allow that it could live because there is an old superstition that if the Mother dies within a certain time the baby dies also.

Poor Raven! She showed so much unselfishness and kind thoughtfulness of others during and before her illness. She leaves six little children to mourn a most devoted and affectionate Mother. It is another in the long list of Yankee enormities for which surely a heavy retribution must come some day. "Our God will come and keep no more misconstrued silence as before."

I don't think I can pretend to tell you anything of the days after you left and after the Yankees entered. Wednesday and Thursday were visionary days. There was a wild hurrying to and fro, pale agitated faces, intolerable anxiety, painful rumours, shelling of the town, cannonading advancing and then receding. At times musketry firing was distinctly heard. We thought that nothing could be worse. Alas, we little knew what fate had in store for us. On Friday morning we were awakened by a long, deep, thundering roar, which shook the house. We knew that it was the blowing up which had begun, and that the evacuation had commenced. A message came from Mr. Smith for Langdon to go at once and off he went, calm and quiet as usual.[8] We all got up and prepared for the agitations of the day. Troops were passing by and we chatted with and breakfasted with some of them. Then seeing a group at the Prestons' gate, we went there and had the pleasure of seeing the dragoons gallop up—a beautiful sight. So fine looking and well dressed, their horses well groomed. Altogether the most beautiful moral and military sight I have ever seen. Several of them wheeled their horses up to Alice and had a long chat with her.[9] Young Wade Hampton came across to ask Cousin Caroline something and told us we would have no annoyance from the Yankees, that they would remain three days, and do no harm, be very civil and go off. Still Alice's friends looked a little melancholy. We went home and Julius Pringle, seeing us on the upper piazza, rode up to say the Yankees were passing in Main Street at the head of Blanding. He rode off and our pickets on their horses like statues alone remained at the meeting of the streets to watch Yankee proceeding. Then the Yankee pickets rode up. Shots were fired, a few men of ours ran to their horses at the railroad, holding their heads down so that the fences might protect them. Then came blue coated men galloping about and thundered in the door of the stable yard. Poor Ladybird, such a good faithful creature, was carried off. Julia's pony was an Indian one and most ingenious.[10] Went lame whenever the Yankees looked at her and so was saved.

In the midst of the hubbub, we saw Aunt Eweretta quietly walking to Lizzie's, where they were to stay.[11] Presently there was some confusion over there and Aunt Eweretta walked out with her bonnet. It seems that an awful looking ruffian knocked at the back door and demanded admittance. She and Lizzie opened the door. He immediately snatched Aunt E's watch. She said, "Stop! I will give it to you," and taking it off handed it to him. Then she went off to ask for a guard, for our written papers have been entirely disregarded. First she got hold of a Missouri officer, who said half of his relations were on the Southern side and he felt strongly for us, but he could do nothing because he was going across the river to join his corps. Then Aunt Eweretta got hold of a Colonel Ross, a stiff, sarcastic, supercilious, snobbish looking man with Philadelphia printed upon every lineament and garment. He promised to stay himself at Lizzie's and to send his orderly to us, and in the late afternoon his orderly Mr. Ward, went over to Lizzie's, and his corporal, Mr. Morris, came to us. When Colonel Ross came Julia was so taken aback at his appearance, he having said that he was going to Lizzie's that she never asked him in, & I doubt not he went off very angry, for whenever he met Julia again he looked at her in the most supercilious manner.

We spent the afternoon and early evening quietly. Fires were all around us, but those in the town at a distance and the wind blowing strongly first from the west and then from the north, we knew the fire could not get across the railroad. But at ten o'clock on going upstairs and looking out of Isabella's windows, we found that the fire was raging just beyond the Preston house and all the length of Main Street. The wind was very high. All around us house after house in all directions was on fire. It looked suspicious. We woke up Mr. Morris, tied up all our clothes in bundles and bags; blankets, comforters, everything valuable, trunks, beds, all were made ready. Bands of men were constantly rushed into the yard, after the first had broken the gate and attempted to fire the house and enter it. Parties of marauders galloped about the streets. Not a single guard was anywhere in the streets. We were in the front piazza when suddenly a mass of flames burst out of the doors and windows of the Charlotte depot. Soon it was one mass of flames. The wind blew them directly on Mrs. Smith's house, large sparks fell on it, it was enveloped in smoke and sparks and presently a bright flame rose from the roof. The house next to it caught fire, but this time we carried everything into the garden. Mama and the children, Lizzie's and our house full, were lying on the beds placed there. The flame on Mrs. Smith's roof was put out, but the house next, the out buildings, and Mrs. Smith's fences burnt with great rapidity.

Mr. Morris then advised our moving back into the house. He had been weeping constantly all the evening and very kind. At length he said, "I will tell you the truth. I have saved your house so far, but I cannot stay much longer and your house will be in ashes before morning. Not one house is to be left in Columbia. Do you not see there are no guards in the streets, the city is given up to the soldiery? Go with your things into the garden if the house catches. I will stay with you and guard you as long as I can, but I must soon leave you to your fate. Do not go into the streets."

I will tell you when I see you how we seized upon him and declared he should never leave us. The kind-hearted man was appalled by the fate he believed was in store for us and it was no wonder we were alarmed by his terror for us. We all went into the dining room, which was crowded with bedding, trunks, etc. I went over to Lizzie and told her of the fate awaiting us and begged that they would all come over and let us die together. She and Aunt Eweretta were delightfully incredulous, still they came and we waited together the ending of a night of horror.

Towards morning, at daylight, Sherman, alarmed by the demoralization of his troops, ordered guards in the streets, and every riotous one shot. A few were killed. The effect was instantaneous. Order reigned everywhere, but three quarters of the town were gone. Sherman and his officers say that the fire was accidental!

Let me see if I can describe the part burnt. It begins a square to the west of your house, I think from the street you live in. That line with a few indentations goes about across the town and everything between it and the square beyond Main Street burnt. Mrs. Nat Heyward's, the Robinsons and the red brick house are safe, but all burnt in the square opposite except the corner one opposite Mrs. Heyward's and the small one next Mrs. Clarkson. There Dr. Howe's is the only one standing. No, Dr. Howe's, Mrs. James Heyward's and the Simons' the only ones in that square. In Hal's square only one opposite the Manigaults' was burnt. Beyond Mr. Crawford's everything's burned. His was saved with difficulty. Dr. Palmer's church stands, but everything to the North and two squares to the East was burnt. Then everything to the west of the College and College Chapel, in fact the greater part of the town.

The soldiers rushed about with pots of turpentine in one hand and pine sticks in the other. Others had bundles of straw and lightwood torches. They say that in the burnt district the scenes were fearful with the drunken soldiery and helpless women and children. No words can paint the awfulness of the scene. The men we saw told us that it was the most appalling night in their experience of war. The better men and officers were ashamed of themselves before morning. They said, "This is a perfect Hell!" "What a fiendish piece of work" and such like expressions.

I think that that night's work will be a cleaving curse to them all their lives. The next day was nearly as bad. Order was restored, but it was generally believed that the rest of the town would go that night. We were wearied with the sleeplessness and anxieties of the night before and anticipations of the night to come and the days without food or shelter that would follow.

Mr. Morris advised us to go to our friends and that he would take care of the house for as long as he could. So we are off to spend the night with Cousin Caroline. Mama and Julia later returned to our house and we half sat, half lay down at Cousin

The burning of Columbia as sketched by William Waud, 1865. *Library of Congress.*

Caroline's, weary and worn to the last degree. At dawn we came home and going to bed, got a little rest. This was Sunday, but it never occurred to me what day it was. We patiently waited for our fate. Raven Lewis came in to see us. We had a long talk with Mr. Ward who had been kind to us. In the afternoon I went with Aunt Eweretta to see Hal. She told us of her night, when she bravely battled with hundreds of drunken ruffians. Our adventures sank into nothingness compared with hers. At one time she had forty men in the house, breaking open, stealing and destroying. She must one day describe her trials to you. She says that she never felt a moment's fear. On one occasion she could not help laughing at finding herself lighting a man to steal all her things from the closet. He made a heap of them in the middle of the floor and then stirred his heel around in them. She had unfortunately stuck a bottle of physic with a trunk of caps. They pulled out the cork and poured the physic on the caps. All the Rutledge's trunks were rifled.

Thursday, March 2

It is time to end my letter and send it off. Hal said she would send me a note to enclose so I will spare you her adventures. She is a brave woman. I have told you of an officer passing her and bowing. She returned the bow and he said he had heard of what she had undergone, and added, "Madam, the men of Carolina are brave, but the women are heroes." We talked with several of the Yankees. Some of them quite intelligent men, but so infinitely below ours. Alice said after seeing and talking to them she felt that our men could never be beaten. Hal on the contrary thought many of them our superior but I think she makes a very common mistake, that of supposing simplicity to be allied to no want of intelligence, when on the contrary it is the accomplishment of true superiority.

Every man we spoke to said he meant to settle in the South after the war. They all "liked the climate and the people." As for the women, they said the women in Carolina were the "pluckiest, the bravest, the most outspoken" they had met in the South and they said, "We admire it so much." And, my dear, they evidently enjoyed it.

Isabella kept one young man dancing with rage all the time, she shot so many painted arrows at him. There was only one man of whom I was afraid—afraid that Isabella, Alice and the others were going too far. He was a tall, striking looking Western man with Grecian features, eyes that looked charged with thunder and lightning, and such a strong frame. He was in dead earnest and occasionally at Alice's sallies he looked at her as if might suddenly seize her and wring her neck like a sparrow's. He said that they meant to kill out all our men and then, the war being over, he would settle in Savannah; that the Southern women would then have to marry them. He looked angry, or rather fiery when informed that no South Carolina woman would demean herself by marrying a Northern man. "What will become of you then?" said he, turning to Alice. "We will die," said Alice, "or form an army of women."

I wish you could have seen the mingled expression of scorn, tenderness and humour that came into his very handsome eyes as he looked at Alice and said, "I should like to meet an army of women." He had stopped at the gate to tell Mr. Crane who was standing on our steps as I told you (the morning that they went) that he had found such a nice buggy but no harness. He came in and joined the group on the piazza, and asking for water, went in and saw Julia's harness. He at once rushed up to it and said, "Ah! Here's just what I want." Whilst getting the water, Julia ran away and hid it before he went. He came up to her and said, "You did not think I was going to steal your harness?"

Horror stricken as they all were about our awful night, I do not think any of them except Mr. Morris appreciated our feelings on the subject. He turned to me with the tears on his face when the house next to Mr. Smith's was burning and said, "If I saw any rebels burning down my home as all of you are seeing us burning down yours, I would hate them all my lifetime, and never afterwards give quarter to them in battle. I would kill all of them."

They all professed to think that the war was soon to be over and that we should be friends. "Are we not brothers?" said the tall Western man. "Verily brothers," said Julia, "to burn down our homes." (Hers was burnt down with all Cousin Alice's pretty things in it and everything that Julia owned except one trunk of clothes for her entire family.)

"Brothers!" exclaimed Eweretta, "very different relations, if you please." Isabella and Alice threw in their darts. The Western man's face gleamed with rage, Mr. Crane danced again. He kept walking backwards and forwards on the lowest step whilst the Western man stood leaning against the post by Alice's chair. Alice whispered to me, "What would our men think if they rode up and saw the group." But I was sure that if they had heard they would have been satisfied. They received the most nauseous doses of truth gilded with smiles.

We knew that our church, the graves of our dead, our beloved homes, all our past life was in the hands of our bitterest enemies, but we were determined that they should see no signs of regret or faltering.

"We mean to destroy your food," said they. "Very well," said Isabella, "we will live on acorns." When they told Lizzie Ravenel that they meant to destroy our homes and food, "the women of Virginia have lived in the woods for three years, I believe. We can do as well as they," was her calm answer.

The booty they got here was enormous. I am so sorry for Lise and Sally.[12] All their trunks at Hal's were rifled, and also the one at your house. Only the one here was saved. And Sally's most valuable trunk was out at the Charlotte Depot before the Yankees came. They took away the blankets from your servants and cutting up Sally's carpet gave them parts of it to replace them. Lise wrote to Hal that she had determined to remain at Hampton with the Richard Lowndeses if the Yankees went there her father would stay with them and Mr. Lowndes come away. All that part of the country must have been taken by surprise, and we feel anxious about Papa and Cousin Izard and many friends and neighbours. Poor Charleston! How is the mighty fallen! It is said here that that portion of it from the North Eastern Railroad to Calhoun and Meeting Streets is gone. Louise we think may have been in town and perhaps Mrs. Vanderhorst. How long are we to remain without knowledge of the outside world and so many friends? It is like revolutionary times. And oh! why does not Johnston smash up Sherman? If our men had only been here on Friday night I am sure that they would have the strength to annihilate him.

Rumours are afloat that Foster with his negro troops are on their way up here. We all agree that another three days of them would put us in our graves, and Foster in double quick time. But I don't see what object they would have on coming, and so shall not yet expect them.

In writing to Livy, pray mention that a man (name unknown) to whom we went for a food ticket this morning showed us Mr. Blake's two pictures, one the portraits of Mrs. Blake and Mrs. Rutledge, the other of Mrs. Arthur Heyward, quite safe, and said that Mr. Blake's title deeds were also safe. We wished him to be advised of the fact.

Here it is said that Mr. Aiken is the Yankee mayor of Charleston! But so many things are said and so few are true, that I believe nothing. The destruction of things at the Charlotte Depot was great. Mrs. Wms. Middleton's letters directed to Miss Susan Pringle Smith have been blowing about the town. Mary Manigault showed me two which had been picked up at the Seminary out of numbers in Lucy's hand and postmarked Georgetown. Mr. Smith must have lost several trunks Lizzie fears. Silver, china, every kind of valuable was taken off from the Depot before the Yankees came. I hope that got off your things in safety. When are you coming back again?

You will be in despair when you see the desolation here. The library fortunately was saved. Mr. Toomer Porter went to Sherman to beg him to spare it. He answered, "Far from destroying books, I will send them here. If there had been a few more books in this part of the world there would not have been all this difficulty."!!! His overbearing impudence is said to have been beyond words to describe.

Alfred Huger's Letter

Lieutenant Colonel George Ward Nichols was one of General Sherman's staff officers. His war memoir, *The Story of the Great March*, came out in 1865, and two years later, Nichols met "Wild Bill" Hickok (James Butler Hickok) and published a story about this Old West folk hero in *Harper's New Monthly Magazine*. The article made Hickok famous but was widely criticized for false and exaggerated accounts of the exploits of Wild Bill.

In 1866, Nichols published an article in the same magazine titled "The Burning of Columbia." In it, he not only laid the principal blame for the calamity on Confederate general Wade Hampton, but he also suggested that most of the pillage of the city had been committed by Confederate cavalrymen under the command of General Joseph Wheeler. Wheeler's men did reportedly take some provisions from Columbia stores just before the Confederate forces evacuated, but the overwhelming majority of the pillage, especially that of defenseless citizens, was carried out by Union troops. There is overwhelming evidence—most of it eyewitness testimony—that Sherman's soldiers began stealing and pillaging from the moment they broke ranks in the city. This sacking of Columbia went on all day as well as during the night of the fire and into the following day.

In his article "The Burning of Columbia," Nichols described a conversation he had the night of the fire with a Mr. Huger, "a well known citizen of South Carolina," and claimed that Huger confirmed to him that Wheeler's men had been pillaging Columbia. It turns out that this "well known citizen" was Alfred Huger (1788–1872), the postmaster of Charleston, who was in

Columbia in February 1865 with his family. In August 1866, when Huger found out about Nichols's article, he wrote a response to the editor of the *New York World*, denying, among other things, that the conversation reported by Nichols ever took place.

THE BURNING OF COLUMBIA
Letter from Hon. Alfred Huger
Charleston, S.C., August 22 [1866]

To the Editor of the World.

SIR: I most unwillingly leave the retirement and obscurity which old age and circumstances have provided; but a remark in your paper of the 13th seems to demand it. A writer signed "S," replying to an article in Harper's Magazine for August, introduces my name in these words: "This must refer to Alfred Huger, for many years postmaster at Charleston," &c. &c. I turn to the Magazine, and to my surprise I find a contributor, whose purposes and motives it is not my business to define, making capital out of so barren a subject as myself. Beginning with the "Burning of Columbia," and the abuse of General Hampton, he says: "Among others to whom I was sent to give assistance was Mr. Huger, a well known citizen of South Carolina," and then recounts an elaborate conversation about a band of thieves calling themselves Wheeler's cavalry, &c., and in another part of his narrative writes: "When the citizens of Columbia begin their investigations of the burning of that city, and the pillaging of houses and robbing of citizens, let them not forget to take evidence of Mr. Huger!" I am thus put on the stand without being consulted, and shall commence by saying that if this individual or any other was ever "sent" to my "assistance," the mission has been strangely disregarded. I never saw any such person as he claims to be, though I was an eyewitness to the burning of Columbia. I never had any such intercourse with any human being

George W. Nichols and "Wild Bill," an illustration from Nichols's 1867 article. *Wikimedia Commons.*

in General Sherman's army, or out of it; and if investigations are made and the evidence of Mr. Huger is called for, I shall, with a deep consciousness of what is due to truth, say that, before Almighty God, all that I saw, all that I heard, all that I suffered, all that I believe, is in direct opposition to what is affirmed by the writer for Harper's Magazine, and from which he quotes Mr. Huger as a portion of his authority; and I ask leave to add, after maturely reflecting upon the events of that fearful night, when every feeling of humanity seemed to be obliterated, if my "well-being" here and hereafter depended on the accuracy of my statement, I would say that the precision, order, method and discipline which prevailed from the entrance of the federal army to its departure, could only emanate from military authority. How could I come to any other conclusion with the fact, regarded as indisputable, that the city was doomed before it was taken? And that as the tragedy progressed, everybody saw the programme carried out, as they had previously expected? Or how am I to believe the evidence of my own senses when an individual pretending to be an officer, talks of burning the city, pillaging houses, robbing citizens, &c. as if "these" were unfounded charges? Why, sir, I never supposed I was dealt with more hardly than others, because I knew that the "plunder" was universal. Yet Mr. Huger who is to bear witness for one who was sent to assist him, now declares that he was mercilessly robbed; that his person was ruthlessly violated; that food was taken away from his orphan children, and that his family were brutally insulted by well mounted and well armed men in the uniform of the United States! For aught I know, it may be usual or even necessary to grant this license, while the denial is equally absurd and wicked, and the attempt to implicate other people in the consummation of both! But this is the end that such things come to, and the natural consequence of calling witnesses to prove what the witnesses themselves know to be false. I saw those who were apparently plying their vocation deliberately set fire to houses, carrying with them combustible preparations for doing so. Of the effort made to prevent them I say nothing, because I saw nothing. It gratifies me, however, to relate this instance of kindness. My own house was about to be destroyed by the firing of an adjoining building. There were two western men looking on—soldiers in the true sense of the word. I asked one of them (their names were Elliott and Goodman, one

General Wade Hampton of South Carolina. *Wikimedia Commons.*

from Indiana, the other from Iowa), "Have you a family at home?" The man showed that he had a heart, and, as the incendiary moved off to other subjects, he did assist me, without being "sent," and with my servants, and the only child big enough to "hand a bucket," we saved the house, with its helpless inmates, thanks to the Good Samaritan.

My conviction is that Columbia was cruelly and uselessly sacked and burned, without resistance, after being in complete possession of General Sherman's army; but who gave the "order" to apply the torch is not one for the victims either to know or to care. Hundreds of helpless women and children were turned out to their fate. It is the historian's business to find evidence to meet the case, not mine, and my voice would never have been heard had I not been unjustly dragged before the public. The "truth," and the "whole truth," will probably never appear; but it is "recorded in the high chancery of Heaven," where no power can make the erasure.

Mr. Editor, I crave your patience a little longer, and beg your attention to the first sentence of the article of which I complain. It reads thus: "If Mr. Wade Hampton is anxious to add a deeper shame to a dishonored name, he has attained that end and by his renewed attempts to hold General Sherman responsible for the burning of Columbia and its terrible consequences," &c. Now, sir, I speak for every honest man between the mountains and the seacoast, and between the Savannah river and the Peedee, when I say, "If this opinion and this epithet are not equally revolting and insulting, then the common sensibilities of nature are made extinct by the sufferings we have endured." If "Hampton" is a "dishonored name," then there is none within the limits of this down-trodden and persecuted State that can be considered as unsullied. Here in South Carolina, and throughout the South, every human being feels that where the name of Hampton is best known it is the most revered, and he who bears it is the most beloved. Before the present incumbent saw the light that name was identified with all that is brave and honorable and generous. What a noble sire (who emphatically and habitually "did the honors" of his native State) has left impressed upon the hearts of his countrymen as a legacy to his children, this slandered Mr. Wade Hampton, the Lieutenant-General of the Confederate army, will transmit to another generation, bright and untarnished. If there is one among us more cherished than the rest, it is he, upon whom the gratuitous assault is so brutally, and yet so feebly made. And if today, or tomorrow a canvass should be opened for our "representative men," to fill the highest office in the gift of a heart-broken but grateful people, none could be found strong enough to compete with him for their favor. And it would be untrue to the living and the dead, if such were not the unanimous decision. I have said that the historian must find evidence as to the burning of Columbia, and he will find it; the foolish attempt to hold Hampton responsible, is beyond the tether of his last calumniator, and is hardly worthy of a serious refutation. These few questions, when they are asked, will be found difficult to answer. Where was Hampton when the conflagration began to take its regular course at eight o'clock at night? Did the cotton which was burning at the east end of Main street travel against a gale of wind to the extreme west, more than a mile off? Was it not there and then that we were called on to perceive that our doom was sealed? Why talk of putting out the fire in a church-yard when it is notorious that the sacrament silver belonging to the altar was stolen, and I think, subsequently given up? Did Hampton burn the country-seats surrounding Columbia, leaving his kith and kindred without a shelter? Did he burn the farm-house on the wayside and away from the wayside? Every grist-mill and flour-mill? Did he burn Camden, and Winnsborough, and Cheraw? Was the quantity of silverplate taken from the citizens of Columbia sold for Hampton's benefit in New York and elsewhere? Is it the necessary province of war to obliterate all mercy and shame? But enough, when the Searcher of Hearts commences His "investigations," Hampton will be found entrenched by truth—surrounded by that strength, which "prosperity and victory" cannot give, and which "adversity and malignity" cannot take away.

Mr. Editor, we are doing our best, with Heaven's help, to have a country once more. North, South, East and West are enlisted in this holy enterprise. All have joined hands in this sacred work, and a Chief Magistrate, distinguished for his high inflexible "courage" in its performance, wisely tells us: "If we cannot forget the 'past' we can never have a 'future'"; and standing as I do, almost in sight of the grave, among the oldest men in the State that gave me birth, I will say Amen to that sentiment. Let the past be forgotten, if such is possible; at any rate, let it not be referred to if the object is "peace" and the "hope is in the future."

I am, very respectfully, your obedient servant,

ALFRED HUGER

II

The Burning of Columbia

Lieutenant Platter's Diary

Lieutenant Cornelius C. Platter (1839–1909) served in the Eighty-First Ohio Volunteers, a regiment that was part of the army of General Sherman in its Georgia and South Carolina campaigns. He kept a diary for many months, and his observations about the burning of Columbia, which he characterized as "a very disgraceful affair," are excerpted here.

Friday, February 17, 1865

This has been a day long to be remembered. We entered the Capital of the state which first passed the Ordinance of Secession. We rec[eive]d orders to march at 7 a.m. but we did not get off at the time ordered. After breakfast Lieut Johnson, Captain McCain and I went down to Broad River. Our men were busy laying pontoons....We crossed Broad River in rear of 1st Div and went through Columbia with bands playing, Colors flying &c &c. It was indeed a grand sight to see a "victorious army" marching through the "stronghold of secession." A great many stores were plundered and the negroes were wild with delight. A great many soldiers were drunk having obtained whiskey from a distillery. Columbia was quite a nice city. Contains some splendid residences. The new state House will be a splendid edifice when completed. We went in camp one mile from the city—15th Corps in line of battle. About

The Burning of Columbia

GENERAL SHERMAN'S ENTRY INTO COLUMBIA, SOUTH CAROLINA, February 17, 1865.

Sherman's entry into Columbia, February 17, 1865, published in *Harper's Weekly*, April 1, 1865. *Wikimedia Commons*.

dusk the city was set on fire and from then until midnight the fire raged, and as the wind was blowing fiercely the sight is said to have beggared description. It was indeed grand as seen from our Camp. The streets were full of drunken soldiers, guards, firemen, women and children &c &c. All was confusion & excitement and as the wind was very high it was just impossible to extinguish it the flames. The boys were loaded with delicacies. Tobacco was plenty, more than we know what to do with. Most of it was taken from the stores in the city. The burning of Columbia does not reflect much credit on our army. A very disgraceful affair—but whisky done it and not the soldiers.

William B. Yates's Nightmare

William Black Yates (1809–1882) was a Presbyterian clergyman famed for his ministry to seamen in Charleston, South Carolina. In 1859, he established a training school for merchant seamen, the first of its kind, and its classes were held on board a ship off White Point Garden in Charleston. In early August 1863, because of growing enemy threats to the city, the school was moved to a farm near Orangeburg, South Carolina. When Sherman's army moved into Orangeburg District in February 1865, William B. Yates and his family, and possibly the marine school students, were apparently driven to flee to Columbia. Yates was the father of three sons and two daughters, Agnes and Sarah.

In a journal, he wrote down some of his "reflections during the visit of the Yankees under Sherman in Columbia."

> The sight of the burning of Columbia which I am convinced from all I heard from overhearing conversations between Gen. F. P. Blair, who made his headquarters in Mrs. A. Wallace's house where I and my family were, with Mrs. Alfred Wallace, convinced me it was a premeditated plan, and had not Sherman's army left our houses before they intended they would not have left one house.[13] I am however constrained to say that Gen. Blair while an inmate of my residence acted the gentleman giving to my wife and daughters and Mrs. Wallace and infant every protection. His orderly was one of the most consummate scoundrels I have ever

met with. We caught him one night at 12 o'clock setting fire to the garret and he attempted on several occasions to enter the chambers of my daughters, who with more than heroic prowess told him Gen. Blair had authorized them to shoot any one who attempted to enter their chamber.

The night of the awful fire and sacking, I was trying to write some description of the scenes around me, and found language inadequate and fell into a doze, and in that dreamy state woke up in Hell, and saw the devils with their torches dancing around me. Next morning I said to my wife and others I had realized the scenes of last night.

The plunder in Columbia of gold, silver and valuables was immense, 1200 watches and quarts of other jewelry. Gen. Blair bought a large plated ice cooling pitcher which he said his men had brought in and gave it to Mrs. Yates telling her if she could not find the owner to keep it. He also gave my little son an elegant double barrel gun and told him to shoot any straggler who might attempt to insult his mother or sisters.

Ilium in Flames

Dr. Chapman J. Milling was a South Carolina physician, historian and author. Two of his best-known books are *Beneath So Kind a Sky* and *Red Carolinians*. In 1928, he wrote an account of the burning of Columbia that was published serially as "Ilium in Flames" in the *Confederate Veteran* magazine. His title was a reference to the burning and plunder of the ancient city of Troy, also known as Ilium, as chronicled in Homer's tragic epic poem the *Iliad*. "Never in the history of warfare was an army more completely given to plunder," Milling observed. "Venerable Priam, moaning over the sack of his beloved Ilium, saw ravages less barbarous, destruction less wanton, than was the fate of the Palmetto capital." Milling's account is presented here with only slight abridgment.[14]

The task of treating impartially one of the most dramatic events of the great sectional conflict is one of manifest difficulty.

The author has, however, attempted to narrate the principal occurrences which took place during an episode which he considers is treated inadequately in the majority of textual histories.

He begs no one to agree with him in his conclusions. He only hopes that he who doubts will delve.

A striking example, both of perversion and omission, is to be found in that oft-mooted question—the burning of Columbia. The general impression gained from school and college histories is that about the time Sherman's army occupied the city it somehow caught fire. Some writers assert, with Sherman, that

The Burning of Columbia

This seventeenth-century painting by Dirck Verhaert depicts the burning of the ancient city of Troy, or Ilium. *Wikimedia Commons.*

the Confederates burned Columbia. Some admit that it may possibly have been due to the act of a few drunken privates in the conquering army, temporarily loose from Sherman's excellent discipline, a sort of "boys will be boys" attitude. But the majority of history books, when they come to that disagreeable event, employ the simple but ancient device of evasion. They blandly state that, during Sherman's occupation of Columbia, about two-thirds to three-fourths of the city was unfortunately burned, and the student is expected to draw his own conclusions. Most of them leave the impression that General Sherman was very sorry it happened, which undoubtedly was the case—some time afterwards. Not a word is ever said of the plundering and destruction of private property. It might lead to the undesirable impression that American soldiers have been known to be, in some instances, a trifle rough. The modern student knows better. He knows that the men on both sides of the great sectional contest were the souls of honor and gallantry. That is the impression which, it is felt, must be maintained for him to develop into a good citizen. And it is maintained; no doubt about that. Standardized textbooks, standardized professors, carefully formulated mental pabulum, and at last a splendidly standardized citizen, emerging into the open; a hope in his standardized breast that he will some day stand at the helm of a new civilization, standardized through his efforts!

But what of Columbia and its burning? So long has the truth of this disastrous event been either neglected, or palpably tampered with, that countless numbers of Southerners, many of them hailing from South Carolina, actually accept the story handed them as honest history. It is partly to such individuals that these pages are addressed.

The winter of 1864-65 marked the death struggle of a nation born in exultation, but destined to perish tragically in its infancy. Lee was engaged in the last hopeless, but glorious, battles to avert a fate already foreseen. But the death pangs of the Confederacy on the Virginia front were marked by that brilliant gallantry which will to the end of time be associated with the Army of Northern Virginia. There, at least, the sunset of the unhappy republic was glorified, for a brief season, by a polychromatic afterglow.

Not so to the southward. Relentlessly across Georgia and the Carolinas moved a conquering horde. Resisted for a time by the pitifully inadequate forces which were able to oppose it after Johnston's removal, the great army of William Tecumseh Sherman cut its sixty-mile swath "from Atlanta to the sea." That which it encountered it destroyed. From Savannah the commander of this mighty army wrote to his superiors: "We have consumed the corn and fodder in the region of country thirty miles on each side of a line from Atlanta to Savannah, as also the sweet potatoes, cattle, hogs, sheep, and poultry, and have carried away more than ten thousand horses and mules, as well as a countless number of their slaves. I estimate the damage done to the State of Georgia and its military resources at $100,000,000, at least $20,000,000 of which has inured to our advantage and remainder is simple waste and destruction." Truly, he had made good his statement to [General] Thomas that he proposed to "demonstrate the vulnerability of the South and to make its inhabitants feel the war and individual ruin are synonymous terms."

Turning northward from Savannah, the army continued its progress into South Carolina and admitted as its purpose the flaying

The Burning of Columbia

This dramatic image depicts Sherman's destructive March to the Sea through Georgia. *Library of Congress.*

of that already stricken commonwealth. For South Carolina was regarded as the cradle of secession, and as such was blamed for all the hardships which the Union soldier had suffered. Up through the country it came; and when it had passed, gaunt chimneys against the skyline marked where the dwellings of a people had stood—"Sherman's sentinels." Granaries were destroyed, horses and cattle were driven off or killed, and smokehouses were rifled of their contents. The sun would rise on a smiling plantation and set on a ruined desert. Out from their holdings poured the people, emptying hut and manor. Feeling certain that Charleston was the destination of the invaders, the fleeing low countrymen poured with their treasures into Columbia.

Every train arriving in the capital carried a multitude of refugees. Into the city moved the banks with their wealth of plate, but poverty of specie. Stores of provisions, too, found their way to Columbia, for the steadily increasing populace anticipated a long sojourn.

But with all their busy preparations the people of South Carolina have erred. Their calculations are at fault; for the crafty Sherman marches elsewhere than to Charleston. The salt prepared for sowing upon the sight of that proud metropolis is to be dedicated to other purposes.[15]

"By four P.M, February 12," says Sherman in his report, "the whole corps was in Orangeburg and began the work of destruction upon the railroad. Blair was ordered to destroy railroad effectively up to Lewisville, and to push the enemy across the Congaree and force him to burn the bridges, which he did on the 14th; and, without wasting time or labor on Branchville, or Charleston, which I knew the enemy could no longer hold, I turned all columns straight on Columbia."[16]

The march proceeded. Repeated assaults of Wheeler's cavalry served only to irritate the approaching host. The attempt of a levee patrol to dam with shovels the angry Mississippi would have been equally effectual. Like a bed of molten lava gradually engulfing the forest at the foot of Vesuvius, it moved. The people saw it, and read their fate in the flight of its victims. Columbia, the beautiful, was to be included in the itinerary of Sherman.

Early on the morning of February 16, Sherman's force reached a hill overlooking the Congaree. His grim artillery frowned upon the newly built capitol, pouring shells into the helpless town.[17] Several of these struck the State House, but rebounded impotently from its stout walls of granite. A small Confederate picket destroyed the bridge across the Congaree, but the Federal army, turning its course up the river, made ready to occupy the town on the 17th. The next morning saw the completion of a pontoon bridge, hastily thrown across the stream by the engineers; and soon the long blue line wound up the river road.

The advance was met by Mayor Goodwyn and three of his aldermen, who formally surrendered the city. They were received by Colonel Stone, 25th Iowa Infantry, who assured that private property would be protected and an honorable occupation accorded their city.

"The Confederate forces having evacuated Columbia," read Mayor Goodwyn's note to Sherman, "I deem it my duty as mayor and representative of the city to ask for its citizens the treatment accorded by the usages of civilized warfare. I, therefore, respectfully request that you give a sufficient guard, in advance

of the army, to maintain order in the city and protect the persons and property of its citizens."

Very respectfully, T.J. Goodwyn, Mayor.

Colonel Stone climbed into the carriage with the mayor and aldermen and promised to present their note to General Sherman.

As the advance guard entered the city, the last of the cavalry of Wade Hampton retired eastward since he saw the uselessness of sacrificing his eight hundred men in a hopeless attempt to save Columbia.[18]

The Federal army made its entrance with perfect discipline— bands playing, drums beating, flags flying. But as soon as the advance column was dismissed, it broke up into small parties, which scoured the city for plunder. Stores were entered, and the merchandise was either appropriated to the soldiers' wants, distributed to the negroes, or wantonly destroyed.

A fire occurring at the South Carolina Railroad depot seems to have been the first one observed. This did not take place from any deliberate application of the torch, but was brought about by the greed of a small band of marauders who, it would appear, were loitering about the depot in the early morning, before the entrance of the Federal army. In their haste to get at the stores of valuables prepared for shipment, they were careless with a lighted torch, and thereby caused the explosion of several kegs of powder. It is estimated that more than thirty of their number were killed. This fire, however, either burned itself out or was extinguished by one of the volunteer fire companies, it being generally conceded that it was under control all the while it lasted.

Universal reference is made to a number of bales of cotton which were piled high on Richardson (now Main) Street, near the State House. Of the fact that some of these were burning during the day, there is no doubt whatever; but this slender thread was afterwards grasped by Sherman and his admirers as a logical explanation of the night.[19] Their claim that this cotton was fired by the retreating Confederates and was the cause of the general destruction, not only remains unsubstantiated, but has been completely refuted by overwhelming evidence to the contrary. Both General Hampton and General Butler testified that orders had been given that the cotton be placed where "it

General Matthew Calbraith Butler (1836–1909) of South Carolina. *Wikimedia Commons.*

might be burned if necessary," but the final order had been given that it *should not be burned.* Furthermore, General Butler deposed that his force was the last Confederate command to leave the city, that he did not leave it until after General Sherman's army had entered it, and that at the time of his departure not one bale of cotton had been fired or was burning. It is probable, as some who saw it suggested, that the cotton caught from sparks falling by accident from the pipes and cigars of Federal soldiers who, during the morning, reclined on the cotton. It is not our purpose to prove that the cotton was deliberately set on fire by the soldiers; enough charges of a more serious nature are to be laid at their door. There is, however, ample testimony to the fact that when local companies sought to extinguish it, the playful invaders punctured their hose with bayonets, cut it with sabers, and destroyed a portion of the truck. Nevertheless, the Independent Fire Company, by attaching a hose directly to a hydrant, succeeded in putting out the fire by one P.M.[20]

Early in the afternoon, columns of smoke were observed to the east of the city, marking the destruction of private residences, including that of General Hampton himself. No mention of these fires is to be found in Sherman's report. The fact that Hampton's beloved "Milwood" and other fine old country places were outside the city limits, and that no burning cotton was on the premises, may have had something to do with the absence of detail.

Upon the application of some of the citizens, guards were detailed to protect private houses within the town. In many instances these guards acted with signal gallantry; but it is a significant fact that in few cases was a house occupied by these guards preserved from destruction, except by the express command of General Sherman himself. The guard might defend the person and chattels of his charge; but when the city burned the guarded house burned with it.

It would be interesting to speculate upon the motive of General Sherman in supplying guards to every one who applied for their services; and could we feel conscientious in ascribing it to a sense of military propriety, we would cheerfully do so. However, the fact above alluded to—i.e., that the guards were universally ineffective when the time came for the city to be burned, prevents this charitable conclusion. It is a natural supposition that the general pursued this course for two reasons. First, to restrain his soldiers until the proper time, thus allowing everything to be in readiness for concerted action. Secondly, to reassure the citizens, so that they might be taken unawares. There may possibly have been the additional motive of establishing an alibi as to the responsibility, should later and calmer years see investigation proceedings instituted.

Whatever the motive, there were guards aplenty. And the statement of more than a score of reputable citizens shows that where present they, in most instances, protected the property under their charge—until the fire began. Striking exceptions to this faithfulness, are, however, available, the case of Mrs. Agnes Law serving a specific example. Mrs. Law, on the 6th day of June, 1886, appeared before a magistrate—D.P. Miller—and made a sworn statement, extract of which is quoted:

"When the city began to burn I wished to move my furniture out. They (the guards) objected; said my home was in no danger, it was fireproof. I insisted on moving out, but one replied: 'If I were as safe till the end of the war as the house is from fire, I would be satisfied.' Not long afterwards these guards themselves took candles from the mantelpiece and went upstairs, and at the same time other soldiers crowded into the house. My sister followed them upstairs, but came down very soon to say: 'They are setting the curtains on fire.' Soon the whole house was in a blaze."

Another fact which strikes the investigator is the ample warning from friendly Union soldiers which preceded the burning of Columbia. In general, such warning came from men who had been befriended before the war or while in prison by Columbians. These men, feeling the noble impulse of gratitude, wished to mitigate, in some small measure, the horrors which were to come. A few examples will suffice to illustrate.

A Mrs. Boozer, whose husband, Dr. Boozer, had at one time been in charge of a Confederate prison, had, at that time, shown kindness to several captive Federal officers. She had, it seems, supplied them with little delicacies and in other ways lightened the burden of their imprisonment. They were later exchanged and became of part of Sherman's command. When the Federal army occupied Columbia these officers sought the residence of Mrs. Boozer and informed her that the city would be burned.

The testimony of two men may well be presented at this point as further proof of the premeditated nature of the crime. The one is that of Mr. William H. Orchard, and was given before the "Committee to Collect Testimony in Relation to the Destruction of Columbia, S.C."

Mr. Orchard stated that about 7 P.M. he was visited by a number of men, to whose pillaging he submitted with such composure that their leader was impressed and called him aside, telling him that if he had anything he wished to save, to take care of it at once. He further informed Mr. Orchard that "before morning this damned town will be in ashes, every house in it. If you don't believe me, you will be the sufferer. Watch, and you will see three rockets go up soon."

Mr. Stanley's testimony before the "Mixed Commission on British and American Claims," Washington, D.C., 1873, is the second example of specific mention of signals. It is a graphic story of the manner in which confirmation followed warning.

Question: "Were you in Columbia on the night of the burning?"
Answer: "Yes, sir."
Question: "By what means was the city burned?"
Answer: "By General Sherman's army of United States troops. I saw a man with the uniform of a United States soldier enter the store of Mr. Robert Bryce...with a firebrand about four feet in length, wrapped on one end with canvas, put fire to the store of Mr. Bryce under the roof....A United States soldier told me himself that he set fire to Colonel Clarkson's house. The United States soldiers were all over the city. They appeared to have selected the northwest corner of every square on Main Street, in the city, and fire broke simultaneously from different portions of the city. The wind blew strong from the northwest at the time. Houses standing in detached grounds of from three to forty acres were burned at the same time. There were no soldiers in the city at the time except the United States soldiers under General Sherman....A United States officer, who was a perfect gentleman, who was sick at my store, told me that the city would be burned that night, which

The Burning of Columbia

was the night of the 17th of February, 1865, *and also explained to me the signals which would be used.* I then sent for the mayor of the city and informed him of the fact. While standing, General Sherman, with a portion of his staff, was passing, and the mayor stopped them and told him that he heard the town would be burned that night. General Sherman replied: 'Mr. Mayor, you can go home and make yourself perfectly easy; your city and citizens are just as safe as if there were not a Federal soldier within a thousand miles. They shall be protected if it takes an entire corps of my army. I will avail myself of some time when the wind is not so high to destroy the Confederate property.' He then rode on. On that night, notwithstanding, *I looked out for the signals of which I had been informed by the sick officer,* and saw them. Immediately after the signals the fire commenced at the northwest corner of every square on Main Street."

Another warning from a friendly source is recorded of the Ursuline nuns. During the afternoon of the 17th, a Federal officer, Major Fitzgibbon by name, visited the convent and asked to speak to the Mother Superior. Introducing himself as a Catholic who was interested in their welfare, he urged her to obtain a guard for herself and charges. The Mother Superior, however, believing General Sherman's promise that private property would be protected, did not take his warning seriously. He then appeared agitated, and, in a tone of pleading, sincerely declared: "I cannot say that your convent is going to be burned, but we can't answer for what may happen. For I tell you, my sister, Columbia is a doomed city."

Ruins of the convent, Richardson (now Main) Street, are at the left in this illustration from *Harper's Weekly,* July 21, 1865. *Online Books Page.*

It appears that, convinced by his earnestness, and possibly by the further developments of the day, the Mother Superior did finally apply for a guard, which was readily promised her. A memorandum was sent by General Sherman to the convent stating that he had detailed ninety-six men for the duty from the 25th Iowa Regiment. It is further recorded that only seven of the ninety-six guardsmen were ever on hand, and that these were the first to begin the looting!

But not all the intimation that the city was to be consumed came from kindly inclined Federal soldiers. Threats, many of a most insulting nature, outnumbered the friendly premonitions; and it is by no means an exaggeration to state that when the city finally burst into flames, over half the population was expecting it to happen.

The nature of the signals, so often mentioned in personal accounts, is a matter not subject to dispute. They consisted of rockets, which went up from the region of the State House, according to the direction noted by most observers. They were seen by hundreds of people. The only point upon which all evidence does not agree is the hour in which the rockets were seen. Some individuals claim that they appeared as early as 7 P.M.; others placed their occurrence as late as nine. This discrepancy may easily be accounted for by the excitement of the occasion and the well-known failure of most persons to pay attention to the particular time of any specific happening. When questioned later, the witnesses naturally speculated as to the hour, and it would have been a too-remarkable coincidence that they all made the same guess. It is, however, a fact worthy of note that there was universal agreement that the rockets preceded the fires by but a few minutes; and that after the rockets were seen, fires broke out simultaneously in a score or more of widely separated quarters of the city.

The people's committee reached the conclusion that the rockets appeared approximately at 8 P.M., or very soon thereafter; and their findings should perhaps be accepted as the most authentic, in view of the fact that they collected a greater amount of testimony than could possibly have been obtained by any one individual. Furthermore, this testimony was collected but a short time after the event.

Gen. O.O. Howard later declared that the rockets were merely for the purpose of showing the rest of the army the location of General Logan's headquarters and were sent up by the signal corps. The latter portion of this statement may be accepted at its face value. For reasons which will later become apparent, the first portion is not so acceptable.

Having established the fact that Columbians were not unprepared for the fate awaiting their city, let us now follow the activities of the Union soldiery in the interval of time at their disposal between their arrival and the appearance of the signal rockets.

Never in the history of warfare was an army more completely given to plunder. Venerable Priam, moaning over the sack of his beloved Ilium, saw ravages less barbarous, destruction less wanton, than was the fate of the Palmetto capital. What could be appropriated to personal use was promptly seized; the rest was utterly demolished. Silver and jewelry were the most coveted articles of plunder. Most of the latter was carried away, but the former, being so heavy and bulky, could not be easily disposed of. A great amount was preserved whole by the looters, but probably a still greater quantity was melted down and poured into holes in the ground. These holes were made with bayonets or similar implements, the resulting cast being in the form of a rough bar about eighteen inches in length, and perhaps as heavy as a commercial stick of solder. Many of these silver casts were lost by the Federal soldiers, and afterwards recovered. Family plate having undergone such a metamorphosis was naturally a distressing sight to look upon, but, when found, was hailed as a bonanza by the impoverished inhabitants. Family portraits and works of art came in for their share of attention. Some of the more appreciative invaders were seen to cut portraits out of their frames, roll them up, and carry them off as souvenirs.

The famous collection of Dr. Robert W. Gibbes was a total loss. Despite the dignified entreaties of that scholarly gentleman, his old masters were hacked relentlessly with bayonets; his fossils broken; and his cabinets reduced to kindling wood. After thus demolishing his exhibit, the wreckage was burned before his eyes.

Mrs. Mary S. Whilden, of Charleston, S.C., possessed a valued walking cane, in former years the property of a gallant soldier

Dr. Robert W. Gibbes, the surgeon general of South Carolina, owned a large art and natural history collection worthy of a museum. *Wikimedia Commons.*

brother who had made the supreme sacrifice on the bloody field of Secessionville. She had brought it among other treasures to Columbia, sharing the prevalent belief that the city was safe. As she left the house, her cane, stuck in her girdle, was seized by a passing Federal soldier. But the plucky lady wrenched it from his hand, and, raising it over her head, she exclaimed: "That cane belonged to a dead Confederate soldier who would never have harmed or insulted a woman, and if you will have it, I will break it over your head and you can take it in two pieces."

"Woman," said the soldier, "you can keep your stick."

With as great treasure as was ever manifested by Spanish pirates, the swarming destroyers searched for hidden valuables. Probing the ground, dragging wells, and exploring cellars, they brought forth wealth such as their eyes had never beheld. Even the grave was not exempt; especially if the sod was newly turned, it aroused their suspicions. There was a general feeling that South Carolina must be repaid for secession. She must be made bitterly to suffer the consequences of the step she had taken; and what better way of making her atone than the methods of wholesale impoverishment.

Houses dedicated to the worship of God were by no means spared, nor was the sanctity of his altar considered inviolate.

The Burning of Columbia

The communion of plate of Trinity Episcopal Church was stolen from the keeping of her rector. When he attempted to save it, he was treated with scornful contempt. The sacred vessels and the exquisite candlesticks of Temple K.K. Beth Elohim, of Charleston, had been removed to Columbia for safe-keeping. Profane hands discovered them, and they were carried captive into Babylon. Mad infantrymen battered in the door of the Ursuline Convent, falling over one another in a fierce scramble to reach the golden chalice of the altar and its other incomparable treasures. They could not be found, having been wisely consigned to safe-keeping elsewhere, and filthy imprecations expressed the disappointment of the vandals, forcing the terrified nuns to flee the churchyard, where they shivered during the long night, helplessly watching the destruction of their sanctuary.

Masonic lodges were subjected to like treatment. A sad spectacle it must have been to the aged brethren in Columbia to see their sacred jewels suspended from the breasts of grimacing buffoons who paraded in the streets in the regalia of the craft. Masons in the Federal army made some effort to avert this sacrilege, but were utterly unable to succeed. Local Masons were told by their Northern brethren that there was an impression current among their lodges to the effect that lodges in the South had severed all connection with the order in the North. Such a statement was, of course, absolutely false, Masonry's chief glory being in the fact that it is not bound by creed or limited by section; but the tale was without a doubt a part of the war propaganda of the day.

Nothing was held inviolate by the rioting soldiers. It was a spectacular example of mob psychology. Thousands of men, turned absolutely loose and free from constraint or control, allowing free rein to the universal instincts of theft and destruction, and justifying the basest acts in the name of liberty, humanity, and love of country. Openly through the streets rode the conqueror and did not see fit to put a stop to what he beheld.

Officers there were in plenty, but few were *apparent* among the looters. Most of them stood about and complacently watched. Some few there were who did their best to curb the violence which was taking place everywhere about them; in several instances driving off parties of soldiers and helping to rescue property. In one specific case a captain of infantry assisted a family in moving an invalid daughter into the street when their home was fired. But, sad to relate, such examples of knightliness were rare....

In the old Preston House on Blanding Street there are some rare old pictures and several fine pieces of statuary. This great hall was one of the few houses which escaped the burning, being reserved for the headquarters of Maj. Gen. John A. Logan. When the invaders entered it, they were, therefore, careful not to destroy the works of art—General Logan himself was a lover of the beautiful—but the temptation was too great to refrain from having a few harmless pranks. And so the jovial occupants penciled mustachios upon the lips of the old cavaliers, robed the statues in fine raiment, and arrayed the old hall in holiday attire.

The negro servants were told by every soldier they met, that they were free. Some believed it. Hundreds went away with the army. With the wholesale breaking open of stores the negroes suddenly found themselves the possessors of heterogeneous wealth. Rushing home, they snatched washtubs, gunny sacks, and wooden pails, and returned to the scene of activity. The Federal soldiers, generous with other people's property, filled these to overflowing, and a strange collection they acquired. Groceries, patent medicines, toys, tinsel, jewelry, candy (such as could be had in Columbia in 1865), and bolts of cloth. Molasses was loosely poured into gaudy china vases. Hoisting their tubs upon their heads, the negroes marched homeward and in many instances placed their treasures at the disposal of their "white folks," a strange commentary upon the cruel relation known, at the North, to have existed between master and slave!

Mrs. A.E. Davis, of Camden, records that her domestics brought in "portraits, engravings, mirrors, a miniature, china, glass, books—everything that took their fancy—and we were invited to take what we pleased." The negroes, it appears, were told that they were receiving their wages for years of unpaid toil. Strange to relate, however, these generous friends of the "colored people" did not invariably assume the role of Santa Claus. One lady has left us the story of how her faithful negro Halsey's watch was snatched from his hand by one of the liberators while he guarded his mistress's gate.

That many of the negroes refused to reveal the hiding places of family treasures was a great disappointment to the men of

Sherman's army. Dark tales are still related of floggings, threats, and torture administered to "Uncle Jake" and "Daddy Richard"—tales of cruel punishment borne by bent shoulders, of disappointed rage vented upon snowy heads.

Of the ones who went away with the army many never returned. Most of the prodigals, however, hastened to escape after finding that the promised "forty acres and a mule" was not to be immediately forthcoming. For weeks they were to be seen coming back to their old homes, so lately deserted, for they had discovered that all was not bliss in the camp of the liberators.

The treatment of the negroes by the Federal soldiers was a paradox at once remarkable and amusing. The Western men in the army universally despised the negroes, whom they regarded as the *casus belli*.[21] They invariably treated them with cuffs, curses, and contempt. The New Englanders, on the other hand, were effusive in praise of the negroes' worthiness. They showered them with favors, patted them upon the back, addressed them as "Mister," and assured them that they were equal to anybody in the world. Here was one soldier who went out of his way to treat them as equals; yet the next soldier encountered, dressed exactly as the first, cursed them vilely and told them to keep their places. Nevertheless, both of these told them that they were free, and warned them, at their peril, to work no longer for their masters. No wonder the poor blacks were bewildered and knew not which way to turn. General Sherman himself professed to be a friend to the negro. Whenever spoken to by the citizens of Columbia in regard to the depredations of his men, he invariably launched into an eloquent homily on the subject of slavery. Howbeit, this spirit of altruism did not lead to the arrest or punishment of a squad of soldiers who murdered a negro before his eyes for the trifling crime of insolence. He was riding, in company with Mayor Goodwyn, in the early afternoon, and discoursing upon his favorite topic, when, hearing a shot ring out, they drew rein in front of a squad of soldiers who were standing over the quivering body of a stalwart young buck.

"How came this negro shot?" demanded the general.

"He gave us some of his d—d lip, General," replied one of the soldiers.

"Stop this, boys," said Sherman. "This is all wrong. Take the body away and bury it." Then he turned to the mayor and observed,

"In quiet times, such a thing ought to be noticed, but in times like this it cannot be done." Then, taking up his argument where he had left off, he continued his remarks pertaining to the evils and cruelties of the "peculiar institution."

The afternoon went on apace. A bleak, dreary February twilight possessed the city. Emboldened now by their successes and encouraged by the approaching darkness, the bands of spoilers who had all day been ransacking houses began to turn their attention to individuals. A favorite procedure was to ask the time of day of a citizen, and, when he pulled out his watch, to snatch it from his grasp. Numbers were thus deprived of their timepieces. Even the persons of distinguished foreigners were not respected. August Conrad, the Hanoverian consul, who has written a stirring account of the sack of Columbia, tells us that he was robbed of his watch by the captain of a company who seemed to be on patrol duty. Conrad was at the time carrying a strong box containing the papers of the consulate and other articles of value. This they seized and forcibly opened, appropriating the entire contents with the exception of the consular seal and a few valueless documents.

This portrait of General William T. Sherman was created by Currier & Ives. *Library of Congress.*

Hurrying individuals, attempting to save small possessions, were seized and their bundles opened. Generally the contents were simply scattered to the four winds or were destroyed, but in some instances were gruffly handed back to the owners after having been thoroughly ransacked. Dr. Sill chronicles a pathetic incident wherein a poor and destitute French woman was robbed of her one sack of flour, the last remaining crumb of food she possessed on earth. To her importunities that she was a French citizen, that she was not responsible for the war, and that the loss of her flour would leave herself and her orphaned child to starve, the brutes replied by ripping her little sack open with their bayonets and scattering her only food.

The Burning of Columbia

Says Conrad: "Everywhere, there were unruly, shabby fellows who could not fail to produce terror in everybody, collected from the lowest orders of humanity, from every nation in the world, among whom, with the exception of the Americans from the interior, the Irish and Germans were most numerous. To the shame of the German nation must I, with sorrow, declare that its sons that belonged to this army were the foremost and most active in the shameful deeds which were done, and of this fact, I had, on many occasions, the opportunity to convince myself." Mr. Conrad was a German, and would not thus revile his own countrymen were not the charges he lays against them true.

The above instances of savagery are by no means isolated cases. Earrings were snatched from ladies' ears, leaving jagged, bleeding wounds. Women were seized and their clothing torn off in the frenzied search for valuables. In some few cases brutal assaults were made upon the women themselves, but usually there was a restraining comrade among the squad of housebreakers. Several such cases were reported from the outlying districts where there was less danger of detection; but in the city the personal safety of women was fairly secure.

And now, as the winter darkness descended, the small parties began to group themselves into larger bodies. The rioting grew more boisterous, the assaults bolder, and the demands greater and more imperative.

It was a wild scene. The broad streets filled with shouting, swearing parties of men. Solitary guards paraded up and down in front of houses, glancing impatiently at the time of day, and hoping for relief so that they might share in the fun; or stretched lazily on the porch steps, nonchalantly watching the atrocities occurring in every direction. Surely, it was a strange sight which met the eyes of peaceful Columbians that night.

By this time the bales of cotton on Richardson Street had been torn open and scattered to the fury of the winds, which now wailed a fierce accompaniment to the prevailing din, a linten snow storm adding to the confusion of the scene. Could the soldiers be long restrained from using the firebrands which they now openly carried? It seems, strangely enough, that they could until, at eight o'clock, the rockets rose. Released at last, the soldiers hastened to apply the torch. From every quarter arose lambent flames, which

South Carolina in 1865

This wartime drawing by Adalbert Volck depicts a scene of Union soldiers searching a civilian home and terrorizing women. *Library of Congress.*

crackled ominously. Hither and thither ran figures bearing long firebrands. Men might be seen with buckets of turpentine and balls of fleecy cotton. Greater grew the fire, and now showers of sparks glorified its barbaric magnificence. Out into the streets poured young and old, driven into that inclement night to bear its searching discomfort rather than perish in the roaring hell within. Gusts of wind now and then carried sparks to the deep drifts of cotton which were everywhere; and these, burning with a sudden glow, were caught up and carried to virgin roofs.

In the fierce heat struggled the incendiaries, trying to obtain a last share of plunder before all should be sacrificed to the God of Fire. Rushing into burning houses, they fought one another for booty; and many there were that night who died the death. Their charred remains, found the next day among the ruins, told the story of their unhallowed end.

Greater grew the confusion, more terrible the heat. Families struggled to keep themselves together. Mothers strove frantically to find missing children. Borne out upon their beds came the aged and infirm, the sick of the palsy, and the woman in travail. Every victim in his flight carried some cherished possession, clutched lovingly some trifling article which he hoped yet to save. Ancient rocking-chairs, feather beds, blankets, banjo clocks, family Bibles—all were piled upon one another in the middle of the street. The tent of bed clothes flapping and swaying in the treacherous wind marked the rude camp of the unfortunates. So great was the heat, and so numerous the sparks, that this insecure shelter required frequent sprinklings with water, even though a light rain was falling. Some poor wretches were unable to secure this slight protection and had no choice but to wander hopelessly up and down the streets in the vain attempt to find shelter. Scarcely a house was left that was not on fire. Crashing rafters and collapsing walls indicated the speedy end of most of the buildings. But here and there an old mansion still stood, the flames from its blazing timbers caressing the heavens, gloriously beautiful in its passing. Calmly indifferent to the consuming fire, like martyrs of old, these ancient residences towered defiantly above their destroyers, until, their massive strength at last undermined, they suddenly crashed earthward, symbolic in their dissolution of the lost Confederacy.

This frightful scene so impressed itself upon the minds of those who witnessed it that, of the number, not one ever forgot the smallest detail. Some of the descriptions which have been left us rival in beauty and vigor the finest passages from the Iliad or from the poetry of Virgil.

"None of us had any pillow but the frozen ground, nor any covering but the burning heavens," writes Mrs. Crittenden. "The terrified lowing of cattle; the frenzied flight of pigeons, circling high above their blazing cotes; the ribald jests and brutal assaults of our drunken conquerors; the dun clouds of despair rolling between us and the pitying eye of God made up a picture whose counterpart can be found only in the regions of the eternally lost."

Hour after hour passed, and yet the people experienced no relief, no mitigation of the horrors everywhere about them. The long night dragged on. But at last, lighted by the glowing embers of their vanquished homes, the Columbians beheld squads of horsemen riding through the streets. At the blast of their bugles a magic change took place. The slovenly soldiers lounging about suddenly came to life, fell into line, snapped to attention, and in perfect order marched away to camp. As calmly as if they were obeying the call to the mess shack, they ceased their wandering. That is, all but a few who were so filled with liquor that they required persuasive measures. Most of these latter were rounded up with little difficulty, but one or two small parties were not found by the horsemen and remained at large for some hours.

After what must have seemed an eternity, the first gray streaks of dawn appeared; feeble, at first, on account of the smoke which in dense volumes still overhung the city. Finally, there was enough light to allow a view of the damage. All of Main Street had been destroyed, but one building remaining thereon. Of the houses on the other streets but few remained, most of these being dwellings which quartered Federal officers. A few houses on Arsenal Hill and in the extreme outskirts of the town were left standing. Columbia was a blackened, razed city, the smoke from her ruined homes still ascending in acrid columns toward the heavens. Her scattered people sought shelter where they could, many finding refuge in the neighboring forests, some in the State Hospital for the Insane, some in the Presbyterian Theological Seminary, and others in the few houses of worship which remained.

It is told that the homeless hundreds who sought protection in the grounds of the Insane Asylum were received most courteously by Dr. Parker, the superintendent, but that, some of the inmates escaping and mingling with the crowd, the keepers had extreme difficulty in identifying their charges, so wild and disheveled did the refugees appear.

The venerable Dr. Howe, head of the Theological Seminary, opened his doors to all who came until, with twelve and fifteen souls to a room, his place was filled to capacity. There was a considerable body of soldiers encamped on the Seminary grounds, and many of these did what they could to render assistance to the forlorn and desolate families housed within the buildings. They

This illustration from *Harper's Weekly* depicts the old South Carolina statehouse after it was burned down. *Online Books Page.*

often furnished the children with corn, and some kind-hearted fellows even shared their rations with the little ones. Fortunate the family who retained a faithful negro servant, for the "colored people" could obtain almost anything they wished.

The night after the fire, a soldier came to one of the ladies housed in the Seminary and told her that the building was mined and might be blown to atoms at any moment. He professed a great love for the little ones and a pitying yearning over the frail women thus exposed to hardship. He tearfully spoke of his own wife and family at home, and almost broke down in his grief at their distress. He warned that, at the slightest movement among the soldiers during the night, they must flee for their lives; and left them to sit frightened and wide-eyed, denying themselves the blessings of sweet sleep, so sadly needed. Of course, the report spread through the whole building and not a mother closed an eye that night. The identical hoax was perpetrated upon the refugees housed in the Catholic Church!

All day February 18, the ruins were searched for melted silver or other treasure which might be salvaged. It is probable that they intended recovering the bars of silver which they had cast in bayonet molds, as an entire train of transport wagons was required to carry off the salvaged material. How much they actually recovered will never be known, for they continued their rummaging for some time. Mrs. Crittenden records having seen them at work among the ruins as late as Sunday, February 19. Since all the banks had been forced to leave their deposits of plate behind, and since the population had been so augmented by hosts of wealthy refugees from the low country, it is probable that the value of the precious metals carried away mounted well into the millions of dollars. Rich stores of plate were taken from the Ursuline Convent. Immense amounts had been left there under the impression that the convent would not be disturbed. The Mother Superior, a sister of the distinguished Bishop of Charleston, had taught General Sherman's daughter before the war, in an Ohio school. Feeling that nothing in her care would be molested, many families throughout the State sent hither their daughters and their silver. This belief was unfortunate, as it would seem that Sherman's men were determined to sack this very convent, regarding it as the choicest prize in the capital.

Before the army left Bamberg, a soldier said to Mrs. A.P. Aldrich, whose three daughters were under the Sisters' care: "Columbia will be laid in ashes; and as for that convent, we are bound to get in there, for we hear that there is concealed in its vaults half the treasure of the rich nabobs of this state."

It is supposed that one reason the convent did not receive the expected protection was because of the fact that Bishop Lynch had caused *te deums* to be sung in the Charleston Cathedral upon the fall of Fort Sumter.

When the unfortunate Sisters and their famished charges were huddled in the churchyard during the morning after the fire, the cry of a hungry child attracted the attention of a kind-hearted officer. Pitying their plight, he saw to it that they were brought food.

Another Union officer whose efforts in behalf of the stricken people deserves honorable mention is Lieut. John McQueen.[22] Everywhere along the course of the march his name is mentioned with warm praise and affection. He so endeared himself to the citizens of Columbia that, when the army left, he was given a note signed by her most distinguished men, which was to protect him should he ever chance to fall into Confederate hands. In Camden, he was again heard of, doing all that he could to make life more endurable for those whose fate it was to lie in the path of his chief. Always, wherever he could, he restored order, drove away the plunderer, and returned stolen property. This Chevalier Bayard fell in a skirmish at Lynch's River, was picked up by the Confederates, and was borne to a place of safety, where he was given the tenderest of care until restored to health.

Great anxiety had been felt concerning the valuable library of the South Carolina College, now the State University. General Sherman had assured the faculty that it would not be harmed, as he felt that "the Rebels needed books." The General went so far as to infer that had they possessed more books, and made proper use of the same, there might never have been any secession.

In spite of General Sherman's promise of protection, the professors were worried. They remembered the many other libraries which had gone the way of the torch. They also remembered Sherman's fair promise of protection to property in general and were by no means reassured at the manner in which it was being kept. But by great effort they were able to save their library, as well as the other buildings on the campus, most of them remaining all night on the roof armed with buckets of water. At eight o'clock next morning, they almost lost their library, being threatened by a large body of Federal soldiers, who swore they intended to burn the whole college. The professors, however, succeeded in holding them off until several Federal officers came to their assistance and drove away the would-be incendiaries. This timely intervention saved as well the other college property, including a Confederate hospital on the campus.

While this interference from the officers would lead to the impression that nothing was burned after 3 A.M., such is not the case. Simms tells of several isolated houses being fired after daylight on the 18th; and the well-authenticated incident of the Preston house goes to show that there were definite orders for the burning of at least one private residence on that day.

About the Preston Mansion[23] centers such an unusual story that it merits more than passing mention. The home of the distinguished Preston family, relatives of the Hamptons, this fine old stone residence was selected as fitting headquarters for the commanding officer of the Fifteenth Corps, Gen. John A. Logan. On the morning of the 18th, when Sherman interviewed the Mother Superior of the Ursuline Convent, the history of which is so prominently connected with the burning of the city, he expressed regret for the inconvenience to which she had been put. Himself a Catholic, he promised her, as amends, any house she desired in Columbia which might still be standing. Seeing an opportunity to secure shelter for her nuns and her pupils, as well as a chance to repay the kindness of General Preston, she requested the Preston House.

Her own account of the transaction, given as sworn testimony before the "Committee to Collect Evidence," is as follows:

"Our convent was consumed in the general conflagration of Columbia. Ourselves and our pupils were forced to fly, leaving provisions, clothing, and almost everything. We spent the night in the open air in the churchyard. On the following morning, General Sherman paid us a visit, expressed his regret at the burning of our convent, disclaimed the act, attributing it to the intoxication of his soldiers, and told me to choose any house in town for a convent and it should be ours. He deputed his adjutant general,

General Logan made his headquarters at General John Smith Preston's home, which is now known as the Hampton-Preston House. *Library of Congress.*

Colonel Ewing, to act in his stead. Colonel Ewing reminded us of General Sherman's offer to give us any house in Columbia we might choose for a convent. 'We have thought of it,' said we, 'and of asking for General Preston's house, which is large.'

"'That is where General Logan holds his headquarters,' said he, 'and orders have already been given, I know, to burn it tomorrow morning, but if you say you will take it for a convent, I will speak to the general, and the order will be countermanded.'"

"On the following morning we learned from the officer in charge...that his orders were to fire it unless the Sisters were in actual possession of it, but even if a detachment of Sisters were in it, it would be spared on their account. Accordingly, we took possession of it, although fires were already kindled near, and the servants were carrying off the bedding and furniture in view of the house being consigned to the flames."

Thus was saved the beautiful Preston Mansion, at present the home of Chicora College for Women.

The remaining time at the disposal of the Federal army before continuing in its march of conquest was taken up in destroying those public buildings which were either owned by the Confederate government or were operated for the purpose of furnishing it support. This was an act justified under the customs of civilized warfare, naturally expected. This task was undertaken largely by the engineers, and a very excellent account may be read in the reports of General Poe and others. The arsenal, the railroad shops, the gun factories, and the gas works were destroyed, and all the railroad engines rendered useless. Railroad tracks were torn up, and the rails twisted. In an accidental explosion, while destroying Confederate munitions, one officer and a number of men were killed.

The problem of feeding the civilian population, a weighty one under existing circumstances, was brought to the attention of General Sherman by Mayor Goodwyn and Col. James S. Gibbes. Sherman agreed to leave them sufficient cattle to supply their wants until communication could be established with the surrounding country. The mayor also requested a sufficient number of muskets to control any camp followers who might enter Columbia in the wake of the army. With characteristic generosity, they were presented with five hundred starving cows, which were too weak to be driven farther along the march, and one hundred ancient rifles. The bovines died so rapidly that the authorities decided to slaughter them all at once; which was a wise move, considering that no provender could be had to feed them. The sinewy meat was salted and distributed in small daily allowances to the populace. The venerable firearms must have been donated for ornamental use only, as no ammunition could be found to fit them.

During the trying days that followed, the generosity of the people was wonderful. Those who still possessed homes offered shelter to their less fortunate neighbors, freely sharing with them the scanty flour and the cruse of oil. Few thought of self or attempted to hoard provisions. Ladies would prepare, at great expense, some little delicacy for a sick friend or neighbor. As soon as the messenger was out of sight, the recipient would send the dish to some one whom she regarded as more in need; she, in turn, would pass it on to one less fortunate, and, finally, it would go the rounds until at last it reached the original owner.

Even with the beef from the five hundred lean kine and the small allowance of meal which the authorities were able to give out, starvation stared the people in the face. Many subsisted from day to day on waste corn obtained from the feed troughs of the Union cavalry horses. This they would send the children out to secure, and often they returned with a small quantity of army rations in addition, the gift of some thoughtful soldier. The corn would be washed in water, boiled and mashed into a sort of paste, and made into a hoecake not unlike the tortillas of the Mexican peons. Sometimes, if lye could be procured, they would remove the husk and serve it as "big hominy."

The negroes from the country soon began to bring in chickens, guinea fowls, eggs, and other produce. These they readily traded in exchange for dresses, veils, hats, or such other finery as anyone happened to have saved. For the first time in their lives, the negroes felt a pressing need for elaborate wearing apparel, and the more gaudy the vestment the better fared the marketer.

Another source of food was that portion of the country which had not been so sorely stricken by the conquest. The city of Augusta, Ga., learning of Columbia's plight, sent her people twelve wagonloads of provisions, generously contributing the wagons and draft animals as well as the food. People from parts of South Carolina which had not been overrun did what they could toward the rehabilitation of the wretched community.

For three days the Federal soldiers remained in the city, and although there was no recurrence of the wholesale plundering of February 17, there were numerous individual cases of petty theft. Watches, especially, were in demand, probably more so by the men who had not been lucky enough to secure prizes at first.

On Monday, February 20, the army of occupation struck its tents and departed, glad, doubtless, to leave such a desolate place and move to fresh and pleasant pastures. Thus, "having utterly ruined Columbia, the right wing began its march northward."[24]

It had come as a swarm of locusts, and, like them, left emptiness in its track. Passing on into the country beyond Columbia, it continued its devastating march, and the inhabitants of Camden, Winnsboro, Cheraw, and many other places in the two Carolinas were soon to feel its consuming strength. A few last desperate stands were made by the Confederates, but Sherman's purpose had been virtually accomplished already, and the vertebral column of the Confederacy was effectually broken. Seeing the futility

The Burning of Columbia

A Currier & Ives portrayal of General Joseph E. Johnston's surrender to General Sherman in North Carolina, April 1865. *Library of Congress.*

of prolonged struggle, Gen. Joseph E. Johnston decided that capitulation was more desirable than having the country further overrun and surrendered the last of the Confederate force of any size near Durham, N.C., on April 22, 1865.

Henceforth Sherman was to be hailed as the scourge of the "Rebellion" and the savior of the Union. Before the completion of his campaign, Lincoln wrote to him saying: "The honor is all yours." But apparently Sherman reflected the story of the flaming capital would not redound to his eternal glory. He realized that there might be some, even in the North, who would not justify the act for the sake of a conquered Confederacy. Therefore, without waste of time, as was his usual way, he expressed, in his first official report, the opinion that Wade Hampton had burned Columbia, "not because of any silly Roman stoicism, but from folly and want of sense."[25]

This claim of the victor naturally gained at first a wide credence, but if few now continue to accept this fiction of war as fact, there are many who refuse to consider Sherman responsible. And some, moreover, contend that he did everything in his power to prevent the conflagration.

A history, however brief, of the events which we have attempted to narrate would be incomplete were not a fractional part, at least, of the overwhelming evidence of Sherman's guilt presented. Two instances reveal his nature. An extract from the letter written by him to General Grant, dated at Savannah, Ga., December 26, 1864, reads as follows:

"I am very glad to know that Jeff Davis is in the condition reported to you, and hope that by this time he is dead and out of the way."[26]

Of course, Jefferson Davis was Sherman's enemy, and as such his death or capture would have been, to Sherman, a military advantage; but the smallness of wishing the death of an honorable antagonist who was suffering from a spell of illness! Compare Sherman's attitude to the noble and generous tribute paid Stonewall Jackson by the Army of the Potomac.

During the Carolina campaign, and before the occupation of Columbia, Gen. Joseph Wheeler, the Confederate cavalry leader, wrote to Gen. O.O. Howard in an effort to persuade the latter to refrain from burning private dwellings along the line of march. Wheeler offered not to burn bales of cotton if Howard would not burn homes. Sherman, in a characteristic letter to Kilpatrick, his cavalry leader, expresses his attitude regarding the offer.

BLACKVILLE, S.C., February 8, 1865.

> Wheeler writes to General Howard offering not to burn cotton if we don't burn houses. I assured him that he would oblige us by burning cotton for it saves us the trouble; that we don't burn occupied houses, but if people vacate their own houses, I don't think they should expect us to protect them.[27]

As we have seen, Sherman's men employed a very effective method of rendering houses unoccupied, which method evidently met with the thorough approval of their commander, Sherman, thus demonstrates to us his policy in dealing with the private property of noncombatants.

It is an interesting study in itself to trace General Sherman's various explanations of the burning of Columbia. Be it freely confessed that we cannot quote all of these, they are too numerous and too conflicting. The several which we are able to present, are, however, sufficient to show that the General was not averse to varying the testimony to suit the occasion. When we add to Sherman's own testimony that of his various officers, what a potpourri of accounts we behold!

During the conflagration, Sherman admitted that his soldiers were setting places on fire, but attributed it to the fact that they were intoxicated and, therefore, beyond control. He blamed the governor for the disaster, censuring him for allowing whisky to remain within reach of the solders. He said: "It is our men who burned Columbia, but it is your fault." This explanation was made to the Rev. A. Toomer Porter, D.D., an Episcopal clergyman well known in the North. Why he should have hit upon the whisky theory is subject to speculation. No whisky-soaked privates had accounted for the burning of Barnwell, Orangeburg, Lexington, and all the other towns between Columbia and the Savannah River. And as for the soldiers being beyond his control, if they were, it is remarkable how quickly they responded to his orders to stop the fire.

In his official report of the campaign, Sherman blames Hampton, insisting that he fired the cotton, which we have seen was not the case, and charging him with the entire responsibility. This accusation was disproved by Hampton, M.C. Butler, and numerous civilians.

Later, at a speech delivered at Salem, Ill., July 1866, Sherman declared to a friendly audience: "We were strung out from Asheville clear down to Atlanta. Had I then gone on stringing out our forces, what danger would there not have been of their attacking the little head of the column and crushing it. *Therefore, I resolved in a moment to stop the game of guarding their cities, and to burn their cities.*"

Again, in his published Memoirs (Volume I, page 287), he has the following to say: "*In my official report of this conflagration, I distinctly charged it to Gen. Wade Hampton and confess I did so pointedly to shake the faith of his people in him,* for he was, in my opinion, a braggart, and professed to be the special champion of South Carolina."

These statements are by no means harmonious when taken together; but it would appear that General Sherman must finally have decided upon one explanation, and to stick thereafter to it, as we find him swinging back to the whisky theory when testifying before the "Mixed Commission on British and American Claims," Washington, D.C., in 1873. In his testimony before this commission, he alleges that the fire was burning a day and a half to two days before his army occupied Columbia! The blame is placed on whisky, the cotton, the wind, and the general carelessness of the inhabitants. The closing statements of his testimony reveal the personality of the man.

Question. "You have, therefore, a warm personal interest in the question?"
Answer. "I have."
Question. "And in vindicating yourself and the United States forces under you from the charges which have been, and which you knew would be, brought against you?"
Answer. "If I had made up my mind to burn Columbia, *I would have burned it with no more feeling than I would a common prairie dog village*; but I did not do it, and, therefore, want the truth to be manifest; that is the interest I have in it. It is not a question of houses or property or anything of the kind."

A Northern writer of repute seems to have observed this tendency of General Sherman's to wander aside from the path of verity. Whitelaw Reid, sometime editor of the *New York Tribune*, and later ambassador to England, calls the burning of Columbia "the most monstrous barbarity of the barbarous march," contending that "though Sherman did not know anything of the purpose to burn the city, which had been talked freely among the soldiers during the afternoon, there is reason to think that he knew well enough who did it, that he never rebuked it, and made no effort to punish it; except that he sought, indeed, to show that the enemy himself had burned his own city, not with malicious intent, but from folly and want of sense."

Having compared General Sherman's statements with each other, let us now see what his officers had to say about the fire—their theories as to its origin and the impression that it made upon them.

Gen. Orlando Poe, Chief Engineer, attributes the fire to the soldiers of the Federal army, but claims that the burning cotton excited them. He says: "The burning cotton, fired by retreating

The Burning of Columbia

Rebels, and the presence of a large number of escaped prisoners, excited the intoxicated soldiers to the first acts of violence, after which they could not be restrained."

"One thing is certain, the burning houses, lighting up the faces of shrieking women, terrified children, and frantic, raving and drunken men, formed a scene which no man of the slightest sensibility wants to witness a second time."[28]

Maj. Gen. John A. Logan, commander of the Fifteenth Corps, the corps which "always did up their work pretty well," says: "The scenes in Columbia that night were terrible. *Some fiend applied the torch*, and the wild flames leaped from house to house and street to street until the lower, and business, part of the city was wrapped in flames. Frightened citizens rushed in every direction, and the *reeling incendiaries* dashed, torch in hand, from street to street, spreading dismay wherever they went!"[29]

Gen. W.B. Woods claimed that the negroes fired Columbia, a unique and ingenious hypothesis which he claims is well established.[30]

General Hazen, whose command did patrol duty when it was decided to stop the fire, reports that "February 18, the Third Brigade was sent through the city at 3 A.M., to clear the city and prevent further destruction of property."[31]

About the time specified in the above report, Sherman evidently decided that strong measures must be used or the men really might get beyond control; for we find Gen. John M. Oliver sent out to suppress riot. Gen. C.R. Woods was ordered by the corps commander to assist in the task. He detailed Gen. W.B. Woods for the purpose, he says: "to arrest the *countless villains* of every command who were roaming the streets."[32]

These officers promptly put a stop to the proceedings, as they, besides the citizens of Columbia, testified. If they were able to stop it then, how easy it would have been to have stopped it earlier in the night, and indeed how simple to have *prevented* it. Is not the fact that they were not sent out until 3 A.M. additional proof that the commander of the army had no intention to stop the fire until he thought Columbia had been sufficiently punished for her part in the "rebellion"?

Gen. O.O. Howard, before the war a clergyman, seems to have imbibed from General Sherman some of the latter's propensity for

Left: Colonel Orlando M. Poe (1832–1895), who was later a general, was General Sherman's chief engineer. *Library of Congress.*

Right: General Oliver Otis Howard was second in command to General Sherman. *Library of Congress.*

making the testimony suit the occasion. Officially he blames the citizens for giving the soldiers liquor.

To Rev. Peter Shand, rector of the despoiled Trinity Episcopal Church, he stated that "though Sherman did not order the burning of the town, yet, somehow or other, the men had taken up the idea that if they destroyed the capital of South Carolina, it would be *peculiarly gratifying* to General Sherman."

In a conversation with General Hampton a year later, he laid the blame on the Federal army. The occasion was a visit of General Howard to Columbia in 1866. He was seated in the Governor's office in the State House, in the company of Governor Orr and Col. James S. Gibbes. Seeing General Hampton passing on the street, Colonel Gibbes called him in, and he joined the party. With characteristic directness, Hampton asked General Howard, "General, who burned Columbia?" "Why, General, of course, we did," was Howard's prompt reply. He hastened to add, however, that it was done without orders.

Afterwards, in Washington, before the Mixed Commission, he denied having made this statement, though it had been spoken openly in the presence of three witnesses. When he was reminded of the conversation, he deposed that he had said that the *Confederate* troops burned Columbia. This effort to back up his chief at the expense of his memory for his original version succeeded only in getting him into a testimonial mire; and he was subsequently forced to admit having said that men excited by drink set the fire.[33] He finally attempted to wallow out of the bog into which his statements had sunk him by explaining that he had frequently stated that some stragglers, among whom were soldiers from different parts of the army, had set fires, and that these stragglers were under the influence of drink at the time. He denied that these alleged stragglers primarily started the city to burning.[34]

Before leaving the voluminous evidence contained in the reports of the Federal officers in the Campaign of the Carolinas, we must examine one more such record. It is the account of an officer in the Fifteenth Corps; a quartermaster, and one who was not interested in making military history more entertaining than accurate. His account of the Columbia conflagration is brief, unadorned, and straight to the point. It is refreshing after reading all the alibis, excuses, and ingenious explanations of the deed, to come across one straightforward account, the report of Lieut. Col. L.G. Fort to Maj. Gen. M.C. Meigs, Quartermaster General. Says Colonel Fort: "The corps began to move from Beaufort, passed Pocotaligo, and then floundered on through the mud and water to Columbia, the capital of the State of South Carolina, which was captured, occupied, and *burned* on the seventeenth day of February."[35]

We have already referred to the "Report of the Committee Appointed to Collect Testimony in Relation to the Destruction of Columbia, S.C., on the 17th day of February, 1865." We have quoted freely from that interesting document. Having given several extracts from the testimony obtained by the aforesaid committee, a more specific account of the committee itself must be given if we are to regard its findings as authoritative.

On April 22, 1867, a meeting of the citizens of Columbia was called to convene in Carolina Hall. Hon. J.E. Arthur presided. A committee was appointed to collect evidence pertaining to the burning of the city on the night of February 17, 1865.

This committee consisted of the following citizens: Chairman, Chancellor J.P. Carroll; Dr. John Fisher, Dr. William Reynolds, Hon. William F. DeSaussure, Hon. E.J. Arthur, Dr. D.H. Trezevant, Dr. A.N. Talley, Prof. W.J. Rivers, Prof. John LeConte, Col. J.T. Sloan, and Col. L.D. Childs.[36]

This committee prepared a brief on the subject which they were investigating, reaching the conclusion which has been already quoted. In the preparation of this report only the testimony of those willing to make sworn affidavits was accepted. The sixty-odd deponents were thus eyewitnesses all. The report, together with the affidavits, was preserved in the mayor's office of Columbia. But the Republican, or carpetbag, government, which held sway in municipal politics from 1870 to 1878, destroyed all the data which pertained to the work of the committee, no trace of either report or affidavits being found when native white men resumed control. But fortunately for posterity—and likewise for history—the report has been preserved in duplicate in private hands and was published in 1890. No trace of the affidavits was ever discovered, however, except those which, because of exceptional clearness of invulnerability, had been included in the body of the report. It is these latter from which we have so freely drawn.

The report of the committee was safeguarded in every way in order that error, exaggeration, or falsehood might not creep into its contents. Its depositions are remarkably sane, sober accounts of people who saw in person that which actually occurred on the night of February 17, 1865. There is, considering how much the witnesses must have suffered, remarkably little bitterness or passion in the report. Its conclusions cannot honestly be disregarded.

Another tribunal to which we have referred is the "Mixed British and American Claims, Washington, D.C., 1873." It was before this commission that Sherman waxed so vehement in his denial of responsibility for the fire and Howard became so disagreeably involved in his own testimony. The deposition of one of the witnesses for the claimants, that of Mr. Charles F. Jackson, may well be cited as an example of numerous declarations which attest the premeditated nature of the act.

"Subsequent to the destruction of Columbia," said Mr. Jackson, "I saw a United States officer, whose name I do not now remember, who stated to me that the burning of Columbia was premeditated;

and he stated to me that he had seen the plan of march mapped out, and that Columbia was marked for conflagration, and that it was a general understanding in the army that Columbia was to be burned. He (the Federal officer) further stated that any statement to the contrary made by General Sherman was a lie."

Of course, such testimony as this, as that of Mr. Stanley, already quoted, together with that of the several other Columbians who testified, was of little weight against that of the victorious general who had "suppressed the rebellion." Messrs. Walker and Bacot, Augustine T. Smythe, and Simonton and Barker, of Charleston, who represented some of the claimants, express it well in the pamphlet which they published containing the proceedings of the commission. "It was a task not difficult," says the introduction, "to select from among its (the government's) immense military force, and place upon the witness stand only those who did not hear the orders given for the burning of Columbia."

General Sherman and the other Federal officers concerned in the Carolina campaign made capital of the fact that the fires were eventually stopped by Federal orders. They pointed with pride to the fact that patrols of Federal soldiers were sent into the city to stop the conflagration. They did not, so far as we are aware, attempt to explain the circumstances that no houses selected for officers' quarters were burned, nor why the patrols were not ordered out before three o'clock in the morning. If their claims were true that they did all in their power to stop the fires, is it not strange that no such measures were successful until three-fourths of the city was consumed? In their own testimony they admit that the fire began at nine o'clock. Their boasted efforts between nine and three must, therefore, have been employed in saving the houses wherein they were quartered, as everything else was destroyed.

The truth is that the soldiers had, by 3 A.M., gotten so beside themselves that Sherman prudently decided it was time to stop the burning and pillaging in order to quiet them. In addition, a number had been lost in the flames which their fellows had kindled; and it was to prevent further loss of men, as well as to reestablish discipline, that the brigades of Generals Woods and Hazen were sent in. Says Gen. John M. Oliver: "February 18, at 4 A.M., the Third Brigade was called out to suppress riot; did so, killing 2 men, wounding 30, and arresting 370."[37]

In view of the foregoing facts, we, therefore, conclude that Columbia, S.C., was purposely and maliciously burned and destroyed by the troops of the United States army, with the knowledge, consent, and approval of their commanding officer, Gen. William Tecumseh Sherman.

That, although no written order for the act has, up to the present time been unearthed, nor, in all probability, will ever be, verbal orders were issued, or, if not actually so issued, an understanding tantamount to the same was received, accepted, and acted upon with great enthusiasm by the majority of the troops, both officers and men, the Fifteenth Corps being the principal incendiaries.

That no genuine effort on the part of the Federal troops was made to arrest the progress of the fire until 3 A.M., on the morning of Saturday, February 18, although Federal authorities themselves admit that it originated not later than 9 P.M. on the evening of Friday February 17.

That when serious effort was exerted, it was promptly successful, the fire being controlled in a remarkably short time.

That the troops of Sherman's command were under excellent discipline at the time they entered the city; that when dismissed from ranks they openly violated the code of civilized warfare in the presence of their officers, many of whom, including General Sherman himself, witnessed their behavior; and that, with few exceptions, they immediately returned to the previous condition of complete military subordination when ordered to do so.

That Gen. William Tecumseh Sherman, having full and complete knowledge of all of the above facts, and being in a position to order, at any time, the cessation of the atrocities being committed, is therefore responsible for this outrage.

That the above conclusions are supported by the testimony of hundreds of Columbians and war refugees who were in Columbia on the date of the conflagration.

By the findings of a committee consisting of Columbia's most distinguished citizens, which committee accepted the sworn testimony of more than sixty deponents, and upon said testimony based its findings.

By the published and unpublished letters, reminiscences, and memoirs of scores of individuals who witnessed the conflagration, and participated in the suffering entailed by its attendant horrors.

The Burning of Columbia

This sketch of Columbia the morning after the fire was made by William Waud, a correspondent for *Harper's Weekly*. *Library of Congress*.

By the admission of numbers of officers and men in the Federal army, before, during, and after the conflagration, some of whose names are known and recorded.

By the military history set forth in *The War of the Rebellion, Official Records of the Union and Confederate Armies*, a work published by the United States government and this despite all the devices employed therein by General Sherman and certain of his officers to lay the blame on others.

By the well-known policy of ruthlessness which characterized the conduct in the field of Sherman's army, both before and after the occupation of Columbia; this policy being inaugurated in Georgia, developed to a high degree of perfection during the march to the sea, and reaching its full fruition in South Carolina, where it was exemplified by thousands of burning homes, impoverished farms, razed villages, slaughtered livestock, and hunger-crazed women and children left in its wake.

Mrs. Lee's Fiery Ordeal

Born in Charleston in 1836, Eliza Lucilla Haskell Lee was the wife of Major Hutson Lee, who served as Confederate quartermaster during the war. In 1884, she penned a memoir of her life during the war, calling it *Reminiscences of Troublous Times, and God's Special Providences*. The central event she described, in vivid and dramatic detail, was a night of horrors she and her family experienced when the army of General Sherman burned Columbia. In January 1865, Eliza and her family moved to the capital city of South Carolina, a place they believed would be safer than Charleston. They knew they had made a terrible mistake, however, when they learned that their place of supposed refuge was directly in Sherman's path. "Instead of flying from him," Eliza lamented, "we had run into his very arms, so to speak." At this time, she was recovering from an illness and also expecting a child any day. The night that Columbia burned, Eliza gave birth to a daughter, Katie Lee. The story of the soldiers who tried to intrude on Eliza while she was in labor was also reported in the diary of another Columbia resident, Grace Brown Elmore, who wrote that the soldiers said that they wanted to "see a dam rebel born" but were prevented from entering the room by Dr. Trezevant, who braced himself against the door and declared, "You'll enter only over my body."

Eliza Lee died in 1905 and is buried in Magnolia Cemetery in Charleston with her husband and five of her children. The following is an excerpt from her memoir.

The Burning of Columbia

Sherman, after his destructive march through Georgia, had reached Savannah. It was the general, and most natural conclusion, that he was on his way to Charleston, as he had threatened such dire vengeance upon the "City by the Sea."

Warning was given that those who could, had best leave the city, and at once. Knowing if we remained, all communication with our dear ones in the army would be cut off, we did not take long to decide what to do, and chose Columbia as our place of refuge.

Just at this time, one of my sisters at Grahamville, on the Savannah [rail]road, hearing of an approaching raid of the enemy, escaped in a wagon with her three children, and, under the care of a negro man, who proved very faithful and devoted, afterwards assisting in her support from his own earnings. She came in safety to our home, and joined us in our flight to Columbia.

I was just recovering from an attack of illness, and still confined to my room, when I had to be taken up and carried to the depot. We left in the morning before daybreak, on Christmas Eve, and such was the condition of the road, that we did not reach Columbia until midnight, travelling all day in [railroad] cars crowded to overflowing. We had sent on ahead of us a faithful manservant in charge of provisions and furniture necessary to our comfort, which he took to rooms procured for us in a cottage not far from the Asylum.

On our arrival, the landlady received us pleasantly, and took us to our rooms, where a cheerful fire was burning, though everything else was totally unprepared. Worn, weary, and sick, we were only too glad to throw ourselves on the bare mattresses for the rest of the night. The next day, Christmas though it was, we spent in unpacking and arranging our rooms and making ourselves comfortable. Being persuaded we were in safety, and becoming somewhat settled after a month's stay, to our utter consternation and dismay, we heard that Sherman was on his way to the capital. Instead of flying from him, we had run into his very arms, so to speak. Time was too short then for us to make any arrangements to leave, besides, we knew not where to go. In dread, we waited the approach of the army, nearer, and nearer it came; to describe our feelings is beyond mortal power. To meet the foe actually face to face was a fact which we had never allowed ourselves to contemplate.

The day before Sherman entered the city, we gave dinner to three soldiers, whom we took to be Wheeler's men, and who told us of the great size of the approaching army, and so forth. They may have been spies, for we got no real information from them notwithstanding our many questions, and being suspicious of them, we watched our silver forks rather closely.

The great army advanced day by day, until they reached the Congaree River, on Thursday the 16th of February, when they sent shell into the city. Through the day, the rifle shots of the skirmishers mingled with the reports of the cannon, could be heard, and the people were busy burying valuables underground, and in every conceivable hiding place. My sister raised one or two boards of our storeroom floor, and with some difficulty, the clay soil being as hard as rock, dug a hole, in which she hid away some bottles of brandy. Fearing they might be lost, she sewed up one bottle in our mattress.

On the next morning, that painfully memorable day, the 17th of February, 1865, we were startled from sleep by a terrific but accidental explosion, caused by the blowing up of the S.C. depot. In trepidation and haste, we dressed ourselves and our children, and waited, in great anxiety, the further development. Breakfast was served, but we were too much disturbed to partake of it, then, too, the enemy sent their shells again, reminding us of their proximity. One falling in the yard where my sister was staying, just across the street, made us start from our seats, and run out, eagerly inquiring where to seek protection for our little ones. No place was to be found, so we nerved ourselves and prayed for strength to meet our fate.

While standing on the porch to see, if possible, someone who would, or could tell us what to expect, Gen. Beauregard and staff, with heads bowed, as if in great sorrow, rode slowly and sadly past. Bare headed women rushed out of doors, asking "what was the matter," and entreating him not to leave them. After riding on apace, he sent one of his aides back to inform us that they were retreating, and that the city had been surrendered by the mayor. "What! Leave us?" was the agonized cry which burst from every lip, "Leave us in the hands of the dreaded foe? Then God have mercy upon us poor helpless, deserted women!" That prayer was answered; for with the emergency, came the strength to bear, and a calmness that only God's grace could give, in so awful an hour.

General P.G.T. Beauregard was in charge of the defenses of Columbia. *Library of Congress.*

Col. Stone was the first officer to enter the town, and our old Doctor petitioned him for a guard for our house, and he refused.[38] This sent a chill of warning to us, as to what we were to expect from their mercy. During the day, the troops gradually spread over the city, entering houses and taking the dinners, already prepared in the kitchens, going into stables and helping themselves to the horses, destroying all vehicles, asking the time of day, and then taking the watches, amusing themselves generally, and conversing with such as would join in conversation.

Until the evening, we had been spared their actual entrance into our house, though small squads had been in the yard and kitchen. We felt like victims awaiting our execution.

Towards twilight, two men passed our house kicking a turpentine ball from one side of the street to the other, and although we had no idea of their burning the town, each act aroused the lurking suspicion of our minds.

Sherman had assured our Mayor, that neither he nor the people need fear, as all private property would be respected, though he could not answer for public buildings. Thus the fears of the people were somewhat lulled, and the greater part of the inhabitants ventured to retire, very soon to discover how cruelly they had been deceived.

But to go back a little, as the night drew on, a lurid glare deepened around the horizon; again our fears were aroused, but the answer to our "What is the light?" was "Only the camp fires!" Nearer and brighter it glowed, until we could no longer be deceived, and the cry was heard "The town is in flames, and we are lost!"

We smile now at the remembrance of the remarks my sister made, in her excitement and agony of mind, when we first discovered that the town was on fire; she called "Can't someone order out the engines?" So little could she believe the truth, and that the [fire] engines had been the first thing destroyed by the enemy, upon their entrance.

At the given signal, in rushed General Howard's lawless 15th Corps, to wreak their vengeance upon an unprotected town of women and children.[39] On came the flames, driven by a fierce wind, and augmented by the cruel torches of the fiends, who, unrelentingly, applied them to building after building as they rushed from block to block, in their fury. The streets were bright as day, and the air was rent with the screams and cries of distress, mingled with infant wails, and the demon yells of the tormenters. Who can picture that scene, except to compare it with the lower regions?

It was then between the hours of ten and eleven, and every house was overrun with soldiers, the whole town was turned into a fearful bedlam. Alcoholic spirits flowed freely, adding to the surrounding horrors. The men decked themselves with artificial flowers from the milliner's stores, and danced in the streets. Musical instruments were dragged about, and strummed upon; the cruel laughter and mocking jeers of the brutes, called soldiers, heightening the demoniacal scene.

Our house was filled with soldiers drunken and sober; and three of the drunken ones had been turned from my door, by our kind old doctor. But when my infant was but an hour old, another party, with segars in their mouths, fortunately sober, burst into the room. My sister, the only other occupant of the room, sprang from her seat, with my baby on one arm, and the other outstretched in agonized entreaty, "For God's sake leave the room; my sister is very ill, and you will kill her!" They calmly surveyed the room, and answered, "We won't hurt you," and passed into the adjoining room, where the children had been asleep, but now set up loud screams of fright. Again they spoke, "Don't cry little ones, we are not going to trouble you." Every other room was upset and ransacked, but surely the angels of heaven guarded the chamber of the helpless and innocent, for it suffered no further intrusion from the ruffians.

Our storeroom, in the basement, was passed apparently unnoticed, which we felt to be God's protecting care in our extremity, for had they entered, our provisions would have been destroyed, as were my sister's. Ruthlessly they emptied the flour, grain, etc., upon the ground, and mixed them with the sand and earth, leaving her without food. She, with her children, came over to our cottage, and the eldest, poor little girl, took refuge in my bed, where she imagined she was quite safe. Oh, for the simple faith of childhood!

About midnight, every evil was at its height. Party after party assailed our cottage, each determined on its destruction. They had cotton saturated with kerosene and turpentine, which, on the end of their bayonets or rods, they run up between the weather boarding and plastering. The room just below mine contained many combustibles, in the shape of paper and shavings remaining from the packing and moving of provisions, etc. To these they applied the torch, and so persistent were their efforts to burn the house, that all hope forsook my brave and heroic sister. Feeling unequal to announce to me, what she thought would be a fatal fact, our kind old landlord came into the room, and taking his seat at my bedside, told me, as gently as such tidings could be told, to prepare for the worst, as the house had been set fire, and that they would have to move me. Two of the soldiers, on hearing my story, showed more heart than the officers had, and offered to make me a stretcher if my sister would give them a strong quilt. Taking boards from the fence, they began their work; each stroke of the hammer was as a nail in my coffin.

About one o'clock, they sent for our old doctor to know what should be done with me. He came much distracted and crushed, and told us that all he now possessed in the world was the clothing he had on. All, all, had been destroyed, and his family had sought refuge in the Asylum yard, already crowded with the hopeless.[40] He advised that I should not be moved, unless the house was past hope, for where was I to go? No one knew. Death seemed to stare me in the face; yet even in that awful hour the "rebel" spirit spoke. "Better to be burned, than to be taken out by Yankee soldiers!" I was not, however, ungrateful to those two kind soldiers, whom I believe were Iowa men, and who, as a general rule, showed the most mercy. But the scenes of that night had not engendered love in our hearts towards them.

My sister had gone almost into the streets, pleading with each officer or private that passed for protection. Indeed, she pled so unceasingly throughout the night, that by morning she had completely lost her voice. Her distress at last attracted the attention of a captain. On hearing her name, he found it to be the same as that of an intimate friend and chum of his, who was a colonel in some New York regiment, and a very distant relative of ours; upon this, he promised to save the house. He kept his word, fighting hard with every new party that set the fire, and succeeding in extinguishing the flames.[41]

Such was the effrontery and impudence of some of the soldiers that in the midst of all that torture of mind, one of them, seeing a sheet of music with my sister's name upon it in the parlor, sent one of our servants to request her to give it to him. We were struck even then, with the completeness of the farce. Another sent for some saleratus, to make his bread with, which my sister hastily bestowed, thinking to conciliate them, and prevent them forcing their way into the room. Some of them said they knew where to come after the war for wives. The Southern women were so plucky.

It was something ludicrous to see how suddenly stout some of our household grew that night; two or three suits were added to the children's clothing, as well as the grown persons, and hoop skirts proved safe receptacles for valuables of all kinds. My sisters were weighted down with jewelry and gold, not to speak of shoes and other articles of dress. One, naturally very slight, with a large shawl thrown around her, covering desks, etc., presented the appearance of 200 lbs! In spite of all this, they escaped the ordeal of being searched, to which many others were subjected.

The Burning of Columbia

I cannot begin to tell of the demoralization of our household; each member would fly through the room bringing accounts of terrible threats, or of deeds done. Our old nurse lost her wits completely, and all she could say, while going in and out, was, "Lord, what is dis? What is dis? Dem debils, oh, dem debils!" Many moments, I would be entirely deserted, and to be calmly passive at such a time was harder than the active excitement of the others.

The loving care of our Heavenly Father was again manifested in the arrival of a cup of arrow root and brandy, sent by a tender, thoughtful heart through all the confusion and danger. I never knew how it came, or who brought it, but it reached my bedside in time to restore my sinking frame, as the intense excitement had well nigh extinguished the vital spark. That Christian act, I can never forget.

About five o'clock in the morning, the order to cease was given. The immediate quiet which followed was passing strange, yet it showed the thorough discipline of the mighty army. Besides, it proved most clearly that permission, if not express command, had been given to burn and sack the town.

As soon as possible in the morning, the inhabitants turned out to learn the fate of their relatives and friends. One can well imagine the varied experiences each had to relate. The homeless were taken in by the more fortunate, and food and clothing were shared with the destitute. It was our pleasure to provide breakfast for our kind old doctor on his morning visit.

Again, and again, during that day, we were startled by explosions which made our house rock on its foundation, and our hearts sink. The enemy was blowing up the public buildings; but our private houses were protected by guards. On Sunday service was held in the churches that had been saved and quiet was observed by the army.

Then came Monday, the day of the departure. The long train of wagons laden with every kind of provision, comfort, and luxury passed our door. The men were splendidly equipped, the horses fat and strong. What a contrast to our half-clad, half-starved men, and lean, broken-down horses! Though these horses of ours, we were told, when the order came "to charge" would spring forward with new life and strength, as if they possessed the unconquerable spirit of their masters. The trains were so long in passing that the ear grew weary of the grating of the wheels, as they dragged their heavy loads along.

At last, they were gone! Then came the overwhelming sense of our destitution! The great stillness after the storm of destruction was oppressive, stifling! What next?

As night drew on, dread of the stragglers seized us, for we had heard of their lawless deeds. Vigils were kept in every house, as very few ventured to rest. The old men organized themselves, and patrolled the town, which gave us somewhat the feeling of security, and God, in tender mercy and compassion, spared us further trial.

Many negroes went with the army; some returned before going very far. Some, suffering from exposure and hardship, stopped on the way, and several died. Our servants were faithful and devoted during the whole war.

As soon as possible, wagon loads of provisions were sent from Sumter and other sections which had escaped the destroyer's torch. These provisions were distributed daily to the inhabitants; my sisters going regularly, with the rest of the sufferers, for their "rations" which, though plain and coarse, were most acceptable.

Two weeks later, my father, and brother, who was on furlough from Virginia, hearing of the burning of Columbia, left Abbeville to learn our fate. The railroad having been destroyed for many miles above Columbia, and meeting my husband, the three walked the desolated road. On the way, terrible tales were told them, which filled their hearts with an agony of dread as to our condition.

Weary and footsore, they reached us at last, and finding us in safety through the ordeal, tears of joy and gratitude coursed down their cheeks. After that there was no event of moment in our lives, except a threatened raid of colored troops from Sumter, till May, when the crushing news came, of Lee's surrender. "It cannot be true," we said. "Lee could not, would not, surrender!" Such was our faith in our great hero. The news proved only too sadly true, and throughout the breadth and length of the southern land, tears of bitter, bitter disappointment were shed alike by war veterans and brokenhearted men and women.

We then united our families in one house, and remained the summer in Columbia. A garrison was stationed there, and many little incidents, both provoking and amusing, took place, but which I do not remember well enough to relate. Our families parted in October, when two of my sisters left for Charleston. The railroad had been destroyed for many miles, and they had a weary and uncomfortable ride in a wagon to reach it. A month later, we considered ourselves very fortunate in securing an old carriage, and in having a much a shorter distance to ride, for the [rail]road had been repaired as far up as Hopkin's Station.

We reached home in safety, and with hearts full of gratitude to see it once more. We found the house stripped of every article—still it was "Home, sweet home," that name so full of rest and quiet.

One morning, shortly after our arrival, we were much disturbed by our butler coming upstairs greatly excited, saying a Yankee officer wished to see me. "See me?" What on earth could he wish? For everything was already gone. The demand was so imperative, and we so completely in their power, I dared not disobey. With trembling steps, I went down. First, though, I must tell of his entrance into the house. The servant was preparing the table for dinner, when he saw this officer and a lady walking in through the back entrance without leave or license. This incensed him at once, for his ideas of politeness and etiquette were very strict, and he felt it "an insult to a gentleman's family." Not very courteously, he demanded what he wanted? Why had he not rung the bell and waited to be asked in? Didn't he know that ladies were in the house? He wasn't accustomed to such manners! While speaking, he conducted them back to the street, where the lady resumed her seat in the carriage that awaited them, and he brought the officer in through the front door, and seating him in the parlor, summoned me.

When I entered, he remained seated, and giving no salutation whatever, entered at once upon his business. Treating me with marked insolence of manner he said, "I wish to see the house, and I want to know what furniture it contains, as I wish to take possession."

I stood amazed, turning over in my mind what, and how, to answer (our faithful servant standing, meanwhile, just outside the door, to protect me from insult). Vexed and frightened, I managed to reply, "I think you have made a mistake, Sir. This house belongs to my husband." "Not at all," said he, rising from his seat in evident irritation. "It is on the books of the Freedmen's Bureau." "That cannot be, and to satisfy yourself, would you be kind enough to call again when my husband will be at home?" He went off without even a "good morning," leaving me weak from the interview. My servant's indignation, knowing no bounds, gave vent to invectives and oaths of all kinds, threatening to kill him if he returned. However, we heard nothing more of him, though, for a while, we expected to be turned into the streets.

Edwin J. Scott's Columbia Diary

Edwin J. Scott (1803–1884) was a Columbia banker. He chronicled his life in a book, *Random Recollections of a Long Life*, in which he included extracts from his diary about his experiences during the burning of Columbia in 1865, along with information he added in later years.

The burning of Columbia on the night of Friday, February 17th, 1865, deserves particular notice, and I therefore quote from memory and from my diary the facts connected therewith as they came to my knowledge:

SUNDAY, FEBRUARY 12. Fearing the city might fall into the enemy's hands, we this day sent a load of books and valuables belonging to the Commercial Bank by W.W. Renwick's wagon to his residence in Union District, between Enoree, Tyger and Broad Rivers, for safe-keeping. We were roused at an early hour by the firing of cannon on Arsenal Hill as a signal for the reserved and detailed force to assemble. My son Henry, Bookkeeper of the Bank, was to have gone with the wagon, but being one of the reserves he refused to leave town, his Captain (Robertson) having notified him to be ready at a moment's warning to go to the front. Mr. Crawford, President, therefore followed the wagon in his buggy. The weather was terribly cold. I went to the Methodist Church and sat for the first and last time in the pew I had selected the day before, hearing an excellent sermon from Rev. Mr. Conner, our stationed preacher for that year. During the day Colonel J.P. Thomas's regiment of reserves paraded one or two hundred strong and were reviewed by Governor Magrath. S.W. Capers shut up the Express office and went into the ranks.

MONDAY, 13TH. Mr. S.O. Talley, our Teller, being notified by Captain Robertson of orders to march, left the bank, as did also my son Henry when so informed. I was alone in the bank, but heard that Mr. Crawford had got back after seeing the wagon beyond Spring Hill.

TUESDAY, 14TH. Busy all day with Mr. Crawford preparing to close the bank. Heavy firing heard in the afternoon about Congaree Creek, with rumors that Orangeburg was taken. About dusk the alarm bell rang, and Mr. Crawford went home, leaving me to send books to his house and carry a few things home; packed them up hastily, and inquiring in the street what the alarm bell meant, heard that Saluda Factory was burnt, and could see fire in that direction.

WEDNESDAY, 15TH. Went to Charleston depot to get car to go to Manchester for corn from Governor Manning, but Bollin refused to furnish it and said the railroad bridge below was burnt. Ex-Governor John L. Manning had for several years generously supplied the officers of our bank with provisions at greatly reduced prices, and sometimes gratis. Hampton reported the Yankees within six miles last night. Fighting heard all day, and coming nearer, but it ceased about 5 o'clock P.M. General Beauregard arrived to-night and expects some of Hardee's army before day. Cheatham's from Augusta, are reported coming; some say already here.

THURSDAY, 16TH. Wheeler's men burnt Saluda Bridge last night; they have been robbing our stores to-day, and several were broken open by them last night. A number of troops arrived last night from Wilmington. The city has been shelled from across the river nearly all day and part of yesterday. Mayor Goodwyn says Beauregard tells him he can hold the place but two or three days longer, as Hardee

This image of the Saluda Factory, a textile mill on the Saluda River near Columbia, appeared in *Harper's Weekly*, April 1, 1865. *Online Books Page.*

The Burning of Columbia

Dr. Thomas Jefferson Goodwyn (1800–1878), the mayor of Columbia, surrendered the city on February 17, 1865. *Courtesy Richland Library, Columbia, South Carolina.*

refuses to evacuate Charleston. The confusion and excitement of removing Government stores and treasure and private families is beyond parallel.

FRIDAY, 17TH. Woke by a terrific explosion, shaking the whole town as by an earthquake. The storehouse of the South Carolina Railroad was blown up, accidentally or otherwise. At daylight Henry tells me that Mayor Goodwyn informed him of his intention to surrender forthwith, having the white flag ready. Going to bank, delivered some packages to their owners and put others in vault; then for the last time locked it up. Heard that the Mayor was gone to surrender, and while at Henry's, over the bank, Mrs. Rawls came in saying Yankees were at her house near the river. Rapid firing continued all the morning towards Broad River Bridge, the Columbia Bridge having been burnt last night. Early this morning General Hampton had threatened to shoot any one who offered to raise the white flag, but about 9 o'clock he directed Mayor Goodwyn to surrender, and before 10 a company of Wheeler's cavalry passed down Main street ordering all soldiers to leave it as the enemy were coming in. About that hour a carriage displaying the United States flag, with an officer or two and the Mayor, drove rapidly down to the Market, where I went and saw Colonel Stone, who had received the surrender, with Aldermen McKenzie, Bates and a few citizens. Mr. McKenzie informed me that the surrender was unconditional, and I then asked the Colonel: "Will private property be respected in the city?" He seemed indignant at the question, and replied: "Private property *will* be respected; we are not savages. If you let us alone, we will let you alone." He was a handsome young officer, who looked and spoke like a gentleman, and I believed him. These assurances he repeated to others in my presence. I thanked him, and, returning to the bank, informed Henry's wife that I thought she could remain there in safety till evening, when I would take her to my house. As the carriage passed she became frantic with excitement, and declared her purpose to wave a Confederate banner from the window, which I prevented her from trying to do. On my way home I saw some of the first troops that marched in leave their ranks and break open Mordecai's and Heise's liquor shops with axes. While I was stopping at the engine house, next above the Market, one of them came across the street, followed by a negro, and demanded admittance into J.C. Walker's store, whereupon Walker handed him the key of the front door, and he and the negro went in. Just then some of them were trying to force the front door of James G. Gibbes's store, where McKenzie's confectionery now is, and in a minute or two the side door, next the Court House, was broken open and the negroes and soldiers streamed in and helped themselves. I then went home, seeing piles of cotton bales on fire in the middle of Main street South of Washington street. Half an hour later I was told that a soldier was in my kitchen, in the basement of the dwelling, ransacking it. Going down to the door I demanded to know what he was doing there. He came up to me and replied that he was foraging. I asked for his authority, and another who was with him presented his musket, saying that was his authority. I then told them that Colonel Stone had assured me private property would be protected, and that they were acting contrary to the orders of their officers, and one of them replied that they didn't care a d'n for the officers but would have what they wanted. They then said if I would go up stairs they would stay below. I did so, and, telling my wife and daughter what they said, I went to Main street for a guard. On the way, Dr. Boatwright told me that Colonel Nichols, at the Market, had given him a guard, and when I applied to that officer, apprising him of what was going on at my house, he called a soldier named Ruble and bid him go with me and turn the fellows out at the point of a bayonet. Returning with Ruble I was told that one of them had been up stairs, searching all the rooms, and had taken my gun. I then went down where they were with the guard, and found they had been in the store room and taken meat and flour which was loaded on one of my ponies. They refused to leave the place, and as they were two to the guard's one and as well armed as he was, he was powerless. Seeing that they were drinking and becoming more violent, I went back to the street for another guard, and with great difficulty, after applying to several officers, found one at Janney's corner, who sent a young man with me named Turner. Turner declared that the other guard knew not his duty or he would have driven the ruffians out. When we returned they were gone with the ponies, meat, flour and some articles of little value from up stairs. While going down Main street to Janney's, towards 12 o'clock, General Sherman and his staff rode up. The soldiers were then breaking open and robbing the stores within his sight and hearing. After dinner I went back to the bank with a negro to bring some of Henry's things to my house. Large bodies of troops were marching down Main street, and a soldier with several negroes was in Henry's rooms. Left them to get a guard for the place, and, meeting Mr. Dovilliers, heard that Major Jenkins, at Nickerson's Hotel, was Provost Marshal for placing guards. The street and pavements were crowded with drunken soldiers, rioting, plundering, throwing out goods from the stores, scrambling for them and making a perfect Pandemonium. They were as closely packed as beeves in a pen, and to reach Nickerson's we had to take a cross street and go around the square. The bar room of the hotel was filled with anxious crowds, praying for the guards, among whom I recollect seeing old Alfred Huger and Mrs. John Fisher. After waiting till near night I got speech of Major Jenkins and stated the condition of things at the bank—females occupying the rooms overhead and vaults filled from floor to ceiling with valuable property of private citizens—begging him to send guards for their protection. He replied: "I cannot undertake to protect private property." In the course of the afternoon I had met Colonel Stone and asked for a guard, but he turned off, saying he had no time to attend to me, though he was standing in the

Market place. Returned to bank and took Henry's wife to my house. Ordered an early supper; and told all to go to bed. Then went down stairs to see Turner, the guard, and found two white men with him, who he said were officers that had just been released from imprisonment here. Begged him to turn them out, shut the doors and go to sleep, for I feared the house would be burnt before morning, as the streets were so full of drunken, disorderly negroes and soldiers, breaking open stores and committing other outrages that I could hard get back to the bank. Up stairs sat half an hour with the other guard and saw the light of a fire in the direction of Charleston depot, on Bridge street. Hampton's house, on Camden road, and Arthur's, in the suburbs, were burnt before night. Just after dark Puryear's, at race track, and Dr. John Wallace's were on fire. Charlotte Railroad track, in sight from my back door, was also burning. When to bed with clothes on, and about 10 o'clock heard fowls in the yard squalling and men catching them. The light of the fire grew brighter towards Main street, and after getting up two or three times to look at it had gone to sleep, when at 2 o'clock my old negro, Quash, woke me at the back door, saying Mrs. Zimmerman, next door, was moving out her furniture and I must get up, as the orders were to burn every house. All rose, and, by my directions, put on all the clothes they could and made bundles of what they could carry. A drunken officer with two soldiers, his sword and spurs clanking at every step, soon after came in at front gate and demanded to know what was in the house. I told him the usual furniture. He wished to see and stamped through the passage in the dark to the head of the inside steps, where, when I opened the door, he stumbled from top to bottom and I saw him no more. One of his privates said they were ordered to remove all combustibles that would blow up the house and I gave him what powder I had. The fire by this time was raging and roaring furiously, extending gradually further up Main street, the wind veering from Southwest to Northwest and blowing a perfect gale. On Washington street all the buildings on both sides had been consumed except the Female College, as far as the West side of Bull street, where Mrs. Thompson's and Mrs. Kelly's were then burning, and the squares in front of me were threatened. The wind at length became so high and the fires in front and on our right hand so near and so threatening that we all concluded our dwelling must go, and, gathering what we could carry, left it in a body, intending to try and get to L.F. Hopson's, East of Camden street. My wife was quite sick and weak, but we reached Mr. Hopson's all tired out and were readily allowed house room. By his advice I went over to Mrs. English's, where he said a Major had promised safety to its inmates. Found there Joseph Cooper, Mrs. Kennerly and some others, but could not see the Major. Returned to Hopson's, and, leaving my family, went back home, where my faithful guard still stood at the front door, as I had requested him to do.

The streets, lit up as bright as day, were occupied by men, women and children, standing or sitting by such household goods, furniture, clothing and bedding, as they had saved from their burning houses. The wind showed no signs of abating, but it gradually changed and came from the Northeast, blowing back upon the fire and saving my premises. Went to Mr. Dovilliers' and helped his wife put two or three big pictures in frames over her head, which she carried to my house, and thence beyond the Female College, where her husband and his mother were in the street. Whilst there Pelham's house, just opposite, took fire, and with Dr. Wm. Reynolds, Jr., I carried water from Dovilliers' well to put it out. Mike Brennan, in Pelham's door, called on three or four soldiers in the street to assist in saving the building, but one of them said, "d--n the house, let it burn!" and they did nothing. It burnt, and Sam Muldrow's next door. There the fire stopped in our street. On the way to Dovilliers' I met a Yankee soldier, who accosted me with one question, "Well, old man, what do you think of Yankees now?" I replied, "I think they have done their work pretty thoroughly this time," and he rejoined, with an oath, "Yes, if you want a job well done put a Yankee at it!" Going back to Hopson's, about daylight, I took my wife and daughter to the front gate of E.M. Johnson's house, where we met Caleb Bouknight, who then occupied the place—at present the Benedict Institute. Leaving them with him, I came back home. Thus passed a night of horrors such as this generation has not witnessed. Our streets and vacant lots were full of homeless families, with a few articles saved from the flames, many having nothing but the clothes they wore, for when bringing bedding, provisions or raiment out of their dwellings they were plundered or destroyed by the brutal soldiers, who jeered and exulted in their fiendish work. The Methodist Church, on Washington street, was set on fire three times before its destruction was completed. Mr. Conner, the clergyman in charge, who lived in the parsonage adjoining, having twice put out the fire. When they burnt the parsonage he brought out a sick child wrapped in a blanket, and on one of the soldiers seizing the blanket he begged that it might be spared because of the child's sickness. The brute tore it off and threw it into the flames, saying, "D--n you, if you say a word I'll throw the child after it!"

The fruits of more than a half century's cares and labors were thus destroyed in a single night, and where at sunset on the 17th stood one of the fairest cities on the continent, by daylight the next morning nothing remained but heaps of smoking ruins, with here and there a solitary chimney to mark where their houses had been. Every building but one—and that a little one—on both sides of Main street for a mile in length above the State House was reduced to ashes, and a great number on other streets, especially on the East side, for three or more squares, were in the same condition.

Ruins of Columbia, viewed from the capitol building, as photographed in 1865 by George N. Barnard. *National Archives and Records Administration.*

The *Phoenix* soon after the fire contained a publication by Wm. Gilmore Simms, in which he estimated the aggregate losses as covering 84 out of 124 squares, including the old State House, 6 churches, 11 banking establishments, besides railroad depots, schools, shops and stores, with the names of 445 merchants and tradesmen burned out on Main street and 1,200 watches taken from private individuals.[42]

SATURDAY, 18TH. Early this morning, my family having returned, Wm. Harth and his wife, with two children, a niece and a couple of negroes, walked in and helped for three weeks to consume the scanty supply of eatables that I had saved. They had spent a part of the night in an open lot, after the burning of M.A. Shelton's house, where they had taken refuge with two wagon loads of provisions and their carriage and horses, coming from lower Lexington to Columbia for safety. Nearly all they brought is burnt.

Great alarm prevails lest the remainder of the city shall be consumed to-night, as the soldiers threaten will be done. As some of them marched up Pickens street this morning, they cried out in front of my door, "This house shall go to-night."

At 2 o'clock I called at General Wood's headquarters in William A. Harris's house on Gervais street for a guard, and was told that one would be placed at every door within two hours, but that time expired and no guard came. Near night, Henry's wife and Miss Gardner went to the General and he promised to send us sufficient protection in an hour, but it was not done. William Harth's guard, a Mr. Burgess, and another came, however, and stayed with my faithful watch, Ruble. I lay on a sofa in the front room with a pistol in my pocket that night, and several subsequently, but all was as quiet as the grave.

SUNDAY, FEBRUARY 19TH. This morning, as Mayor Goodwyn was passing my gate, I met him, and proposed that we, with a few other citizens, should apply to General Wood or Howard for the means of feeding and protecting our people till supplies could be received from abroad. He agreed, and on the way we gathered Revs. Nicholas Talley, Thomas Raysor and Mr. Conner, also Dr. C.H. Miot and Messrs. J.J. McCarter, the bookseller, and W.M. Martin, of Charleston, the broker. Dr. Goodwyn, the Mayor, proposed that he should act as our spokesman, as his office and acquaintance with the officers would add weight to our petition, and we made no objection. General Wood, after hearing the Mayor, refused his request, saying it was unreasonable and unprecedented, but he referred us to General Howard, who he said was the officer of the day. Him we found encamped in rear of the College, near W.H. Gibbes's present residence. He also objected to the application, but proposed going with us to General Sherman, and we all proceeded to Blanton Duncan's house, on Gervais street, where the Commander-in-Chief was quartered. He received us very courteously indeed, seeming to be on particularly good terms with himself, and by every other indication of manner and tone, his supreme pride and gratification at his success. No peacock ever manifested more vanity and delight than he did, when, addressing us, he said: "Gentlemen, what can I do for you? You ought to be at church; I myself thought of going to hear Mr. Shand." Mr. Talley replied: "Ah, General, our church is burnt." He then invited us all to take seats, and Mayor Goodwyn stated our condition, with twenty thousand old men, women and children, having no provisions or means of defense against the disorderly soldiers and negroes, and requested a supply of arms and ammunition, with food enough to keep us alive till we could communicate with the country.

General Sherman replied in a long lecture or harangue on our folly in beginning the war, the subject of slavery, the mismanagement of Beauregard, the condition of Georgia, &c., &c. The fire, he admitted, was caused by his troops, saying: "It is true our men have burnt Columbia, but it was your fault." And when Dr. Goodwyn inquired, "How so, General?" he replied that our people had made his soldiers drunk, citing an instance of a druggist who he was told brought out a pail of whiskey to them. Dr. Miot here interrupted him to remark that he was a druggist, but he had heard of no such case. Mr. McCarter also stated that a soldier had demanded his watch, while pointing a pistol at his head, but the General only laughed and told him that he ought to have resisted. He concluded by consenting to leave us 500 head of beef cattle, 100 muskets and ammunition, all the salt at the Charleston Railroad depot, and wire enough to work a flat across the river. He also promised that his Surgeon General should turn over to us some medicine for the use of the sick in our midst. This, he said, was contrary to usage, but I thought his treatment of Columbia liable to the same remark. Some of us went to the depot, where we found 60 or 80 tierces of salt, which General Howard agreed to haul to the new State House for us. While on the way we saw the gas works on fire.

General Sherman, in his discourse to us, never named nor alluded to General Hampton or the burning of the cotton as causing the fire. Yet in his official report, which was probably made the same day, he charged it to Hampton, acknowledging, as it seems to me, that he knew the charge to be false at the time. I quote his own words: "In my official report of this conflagration I distinctly charged it to General Wade Hampton, and confess I did so pointedly to shake the faith of his people in him, for he was in my opinion a braggart and professed to be the special champion of South Carolina."

Surely any comment on this precious confession would be superfluous, since it discloses, in a single sentence, the character of its author and the length to which he will go in dealing with an opponent.

In his Memoirs he says further: "Many of the people thought the fire was deliberately planned and executed. This is not true. It was accidental, and, in my judgment, began with the cotton which General Hampton's men had set fire to on leaving the city."

Thus it appears that he gave three different versions of the origin of the fire, each one varying from and inconsistent with the other two, to wit: First, that it was caused by his men; second, by General Hampton; and third, by accident.

Which, if either, is to be believed?

III

1865 in the Lowcountry

Contemplating Desolation

Occupied Charleston

About two months before the end of the war, Charleston was occupied by Federal forces upon the evacuation of its Confederate defenders. Uncertain about whether General Sherman's army would descend on the city during his destructive march through the state, Confederate forces evacuated Charleston in the middle of February 1865, leaving the city undefended. Almost all the remaining civilians also evacuated around that time, and their property was left open to the depredations of the Federal forces who took possession of Charleston.

In 1865, Henry M. Alden, a writer for *Harper's New Monthly Magazine*, described the city, contrasting its condition before and after the war:

> *Not many years ago, Charleston sat like a queen upon the waters, her broad and beautiful bay covered with the sails of every nation, and her great export, cotton, affording employment to thousands of looms. There was no city in the South whose present was more prosperous or whose future seemed brighter. Added to its commercial advantages were those of a highly cultivated society. There was no city in the United States that enjoyed a higher reputation for intellectual culture than Charleston, and with it a refinement of taste, an elegance of manner, and a respect for high and noble lineage which made Charleston appear more like some aristocratic European city than the metropolis of an American state.*
>
> *The general appearance of the city was in keeping with the historical precedents of the people. Its churches were of the old English style of building,*

grand and spacious, but devoid of tinsel and useless ornament. Its libraries, orphanages, and halls of public gathering were solidly constructed, well finished, and unique as specimens of architecture. Its dwellings combined elegance with comfort, simplicity with taste. The antique appearance of the city and its European character was the remark of almost everyone who visited it.

But all this is now changed. Except to an occasional blockade-runner the beautiful harbor of Charleston has been sealed for years; its fine society has been dissipated if not completely destroyed, while its noblest edifices have become a prey to the great conflagration of 1861, or have crumbled beneath the effect of the most continuous and terrific bombardment that has ever been concentrated upon a city.

The writer was describing the lower part of the peninsula, which showed the scars and damages of the longest bombardment in American military history up to that time. From August 1863 to February 1865, Charleston was under artillery fire from Federal batteries at Morris Island. Some of the shells thrown into the city caused fires, and before all this, in December 1861, a massive accidental fire cut a swath of destruction across the downtown area. The areas ravaged by the fire were the most desolate looking.

A Union general named Carl Schurz gave his impression of Charleston in his *Reminiscences*. He visited South Carolina in the summer of 1865, arriving by ship, and recorded what he saw:

I shall never forget my first impression of Charleston….As we passed Fort Sumter—then a shapeless mass of brick and rubbish…the city… lay open to our view….There was no shipping in the harbor except a few quartermaster's vessels and two or three small steamers. We made fast to a decaying pier….There was not a human visible on the wharf….Nothing could be more desolate and melancholy than the appearance of the lower part of the city immediately adjoining the harbor….The first living object which struck my view was a dilapidated United States cavalry horse bearing the mark I.C.—inspected and condemned—now peacefully browsing on the grass in the Charleston street.

After the evacuation of Charleston, the city was pillaged by the occupying troops, some freedmen and other opportunists. Most of the pillagers were interested in portables of obvious value, such as silverware, but many Charlestonians returned to find that countless personal items had

South Carolina in 1865

Ruins of Charleston, as seen from the Circular Church on Meeting Street. *Library of Congress.*

also been stolen. Caroline Howard Gilman, a well-known author, came back to Charleston from her place of refuge in Greenville in late 1865, reporting to her daughter in a letter dated December 12, 1865: "My books, private papers, and pictures are all stolen....The pillagers must have had some object besides robbery in their selection. Everything valuable as an autograph is gone."

On March 1, 1865, Union major general Quincy A. Gillmore, the commander of the Department of the South, sent an official communication to John P. Hatch, a Union general in Charleston. Part of Gillmore's letter stated:

> *I hear from all sides very discouraging accounts of the state of affairs in Charleston; that no restraint is put upon the soldiers; that they pilfer and rob houses at pleasure, that large quantities of valuable furniture, statuary, mirrors, &c, have mysteriously disappeared.*[43]

1865 in the Lowcountry

Occupying Federal forces also conducted raids in the surrounding areas, including the Ashley River region. Nearly every property along the river, including the magnificent estates of Middleton Place and Magnolia Gardens, was looted and burned by U.S. soldiers. Drayton Hall was one of only two or three of the properties spared.

Not even the resting places of the dead were left undisturbed. The indiscriminate bombardment damaged monuments and headstones in the graveyards of the city's churches, and Charleston's Magnolia Cemetery, a beautiful property on the Cooper River, was also subjected to vandalism and destruction. Jacob N. Cardozo, a longtime resident of the city, wrote about the cemetery in his *Reminiscences of Charleston*, published in 1866:

> *This tract of ground just outside the city limits, on the banks of the Cooper river, was originally known as Magnolia Umbra. When it was purchased by the present proprietors and founders of the Cemetery, it was a neglected farm, where clubs and parties of pleasure would resort to have their frolics and games. The beautiful situation of this spot, commanding an extensive and picturesque view, makes it a pleasant resort to strangers as well as to our own people….*
>
> *On visiting the grounds in the summer of 1861, at the entrance was a neat, commodious, and accommodating lodge, for the shelter and comfort of the many entering the gateway, the first object that struck your attention was the beautiful Gothic Chapel directly across the lake, and standing on what is known as Chapel Island. Around the Chapel was a most beautiful grove of young forest oaks,* all nearly of one size, *and from the gate entrance had the appearance of a large umbrella spread to invite and protect the weary to rest. Approaching, and west of, the chapel, was a dense forest, which the proprietors would not allow axe or pruning knife to enter, which gave a wildness to the whole appearance of this spot, as if it remained as it did a hundred years ago.*
>
> *Visiting it now the heart was saddened at the change. The fencing around it destroyed; except that of Mr. Reynolds. The Lodge nearly all gone. Not one left of the forest of oaks around the chapel. The dense forest with its old mossy oaks all cut down—gone. The furniture of the chapel, pews, etc., not a vestige left. And in answer to our enquiries found that the troops under command of Genl. J.P. Hatch were allowed to* camp on these grounds and over the graves of our people, *and to them is charged the destruction of the property and barbarity of the sacrilege to our dead.*[44]

Damaged tomb in the Circular Congregational Church graveyard. *Library of Congress.*

    In his book *The Siege of Charleston,* E. Milby Burton stated that in early March 1865, "One [Union] officer wrote that the soldiers near the entrenchments (in the vicinity of Magnolia Cemetery, north of the city) were plundering the property of citizens living near there and that, with the troops under his command, he was powerless to prevent these acts."[45]

    In April 1865, many civilian visitors came to Charleston from the North to witness the raising of the U.S. flag at Fort Sumter. During their visit, they roamed around the city and went into numerous houses and buildings and took whatever they fancied. Even sanctuaries in Charleston were not spared from this plunder. A church historian recorded that at St. Michael's Episcopal Church, "a large number of visitors, from curiosity, entered and

Left: View of the chapel at Magnolia Cemetery. *Wikimedia Commons.*

Below: Flag raising ceremony at Fort Sumter, April 14, 1865. *Library of Congress.*

broke off from the pilasters the gilded and carved ornaments, and took from the front of the pulpit the initials I.H.S., which were inlaid in ivory."[46] Another church historian noted that the interior of the church had been "greatly damaged" by the shelling and was thus more easily "subject to the intrusion and spoliation of thieves, soldiers, and followers of the Northern Army who made free with the souvenirs which they found inside. Prayerbooks, bits of carved woodwork, the gilded foliation of the pilasters, and even the inlaid panel of the pulpit were carried off in spite of the care of the sexton who eventually was obliged to spend all of his time in the church to prevent further depredation."[47]

For a long period after the war, Charleston was under military rule, and some houses and buildings were confiscated for the use of the occupation force and the Freedmen's Bureau. Most if not all of these properties were eventually restored to their former owners, but their contents were often missing, having been pillaged. Freedmen also occupied houses and often would not leave until forced to do so by armed soldiers.

Not long after the occupation of the city, on February 28, 1865, General Order No. 8 was issued, calling on Charleston citizens to take an oath of allegiance to the United States. Those who did not take the oath would not be provided with any travel passes or afforded any protection of their private property.

The Reverend Dr. Alexander W. Marshall was the rector of St. John's Episcopal Chapel. This church was located at Amherst and Hanover Streets in the upper part of Charleston. The Reverend Dr. Marshall did not evacuate with the Confederate forces in February but remained in the city, and after it was occupied, he refused to take the oath of allegiance and also decided to omit all prayers of a political nature from his church services. A Captain H. James Weston of the 127th New York Volunteers wrote a warning to Dr. Marshall dated April 15, 1865 (the day after Lincoln's assassination), which read in part, "It has been reported to the headquarters that you are officiating at…St. John's Chapel, and that you have not taken the oath of allegiance, also that you have omitted the prayers for the President of the United States, which are prescribed by your church."

The next day, another Federal officer came to visit Dr. Marshall and told him that any clergyman who omitted this prayer would not be allowed to officiate in the city.

About a week later, Dr. Marshall was banished from Charleston in orders issued by General John P. Hatch. The clergyman's personal property was

Holding a Bible, a citizen of Charleston takes the oath of allegiance to the United States in 1865. *Open Parks Network.*

also confiscated by the army, and a stern order was sent to his parishioners, part of which stated:

> *In punishing the head of the congregation worshipping in St. John's Chapel, the…general commanding desires it to be considered a warning to those who, attending the services for weeks, so far forgot their duty to their country as not to inform the military authorities of the conduct of this disloyal priest. They are also warned that they are marked persons, and any act done, or word uttered in justification of his disloyalty, will subject them to a like punishment.*[48]

In the summer of 1865, there were not only outbreaks of conflict between Black and white residents but also between the Black and white occupying troops in Charleston. A newspaper, the *Charleston Daily News*, reported in July that the city was kept in "a state of continued excitement" due to feuds existing between the white and Black troops. A serious incident occurred that month between a New York regiment and U.S. Colored Troops in which shots were fired that killed a bystander and wounded three persons, including one of the white soldiers.[49]

On June 11, 1865, a young lady named Marion Porcher wrote about conditions in Charleston. Her family owned Otranto Plantation near Charleston, but at the time the letter was composed, the Porchers were living in Charleston. Marion wrote this letter to her cousin Clelia Porcher, who was with her family in Abbeville, South Carolina:

My Dearest Clelia,

Your letter of the 31st has just reached me & I hasten to answer it trusting this may go safely by Mr Dwight who leaves tomorrow… for Abbeville.…I am determined to write freely as there is no pleasure in writing otherwise and if it is intercepted by the monsters who call themselves Yankees you are not responsible for what your correspondent may say, and I don't care if they do know what feelings they inspire in me, so here goes. As intensely as I have always hated Yankees, I assure you my feelings at first were nothing to what they now are. You have only to see them to loathe, hate & despise them, for they are so low & beastly,

The Fifty-Fifth Massachusetts Regiment, U.S. Colored Troops, enter Charleston on February 21, 1865. *Library of Congress.*

indeed every day that goes over my head increases tenfold my feelings. And to think that we should be crushed by such a people!

They are so truly contemptible & little that it is almost impossible to fear them. A soldier told us shortly after we came to town that we were at the head of a suspected list & watched, & officers have frequently warned us to be careful how we spoke as the city was crammed with spies and detectives. [My] *aunts…took the hint & are very reticent as is papa (though he does explode sometimes). Mamma is perfectly incorrigible, Annie seldom goes out & avoids them as much as possible. I make no secret of my sentiments and have provoked several of them; at the time of Lincoln's assassination many ladies were arrested for not testifying any grief.*

Everything is done to infuriate the negroes against the whites; so far the poor wretches have behaved better than might be expected, that is, they have not attempted to cut our throats yet. They are very insolent in the streets never pretend to give place to you. Several times I have had them to squeeze themselves in the inside & say "look at dat rebel."…Some officers gave a large ball the other night at which the belles were negroes. A Naval officer married a mulatto belle the other night.…Genl Hatch on being applied to by Mrs Izzard for protection against some negroes on her plantation where she wanted to go who were armed & dangerous, replied, "Madam you seem to forget that my object in being here is to protect the negro not the whites." [I think]*…the* [Negro] *race will not last long for they are dying at 95 per week in the city and the mortality on the Islands is equally great, all sorts of horrid diseases such as small pox…*[and]*…spotted fever… etc. are raging among them.*[50] *You have doubtless heard that Mr. Aiken was arrested & sent north a prisoner; he remained there sometime and has returned on parole, forbidden to tell the reason of his arrest or anything about it. the whole affair is inexplicable as Mr Aiken has since their occupation proclaimed himself a Union man and done everything to conciliate them. Was there ever anything like their treatment of* [President] *Davis? He is treated like a felon loaded with irons and the greatest indignities heaped on him, & the idea of accusing him of complicity in old Abe's murder?…It makes my blood boil so to think of their baseness. It seems as though Satan was let loose when such a people triumph.*

Just before and after the war was over, many former slaves left Lowcountry plantations and flooded into Charleston. Some of them took up residences in empty houses, but most crowded into what Caroline H. Gilman described as "miserable shanties." The freedmen camps along the wharves of the

South Carolina in 1865

Left: William Aiken (1806–1887), a former governor of South Carolina. *Library of Congress.*

Right: General James Conner (1829–1883) was a prominent Charleston lawyer before and after the war. His last Confederate command was Kershaw's Brigade. *Author's collection.*

Cooper River were especially squalid and unsanitary. In the summer of 1865, an epidemic of smallpox and dengue fever swept through the city and killed many of them. Much later in the year, "with the cooperation of the Freedmen's Bureau, the City Council created what may have been the first full-time health department in the United States. Organized to prevent disease, to treat the sick, and to establish hospitals for '*all* the destitute poor and suffering in our city,' the Health Department cared for 4,141 whites and 4,953 'black and colored,'" in 1866.[51] During the summer of 1865, the Freedmen's Bureau launched relief programs and distributed food, clothing and medical supplies to Black and white citizens. Churches and private citizens also helped; in particular, George W. Williams, a prominent Charleston merchant, aided with relief efforts.

William Aiken, who is mentioned in Marion Porcher's letter, was a former governor of South Carolina. He was reportedly arrested by federal authorities for refusing to attend the raising of the U.S. flag at Fort Sumter. The U.S. Secretary of War Edwin Stanton had him brought to Washington, D.C., but President Andrew Johnson pardoned Aiken. Marion also mentioned the fate of Confederate president Jefferson Davis. After his capture, Davis was imprisoned at Fortress Monroe in Virginia, where he was treated cruelly.

Some other illuminating letters of this period are found in the correspondence of General James Conner. A prominent Charleston attorney, Conner served as the U.S. attorney general for South Carolina from 1856 until 1860, when he resigned the post because of the state's secession. He eventually rose to the rank of general in the Confederate army and was given command of McGowan's Brigade and finally Kershaw's Brigade.

In October 1864, General Conner was seriously wounded during a skirmish at Cedar Creek in Virginia. The loss of a leg ended his active service, and he returned to South Carolina and spent the remainder of the war in Camden, where his family had taken refuge from the bombardment of Charleston.

In May 1865, Conner wrote to a young lady named Sallie Enders whose family had befriended him in Richmond, Virginia, while he was there recovering from a serious wound he suffered in 1862. In this letter to her he confided his gloomy feelings about the prospects of the country and his own future, and this is part of what he wrote to her on May 29:

> *I have been dull, sad, and I fear at times even despondent. I had labored hard many years of my life. I had won a stand point from which I could see a career not devoid of honor. All that was dashed away in a moment, and even more than that. The very illusions of life were gone. I had looked to the end of the War as a commencement of a new life with brighter hopes, sweeter rewards. In its stead, I find myself contemplating desolation, standing as it were over the embers of a ruined homestead, seeking what may be saved for the comfort of those who are dependent on me.*

James Conner remained in Camden until about July 1865 and then returned to occupied Charleston, where he found that his family's home at 9 Meeting Street was "occupied" by a Northern lady. On August 9, he wrote to Miss Enders again describing conditions in Columbia and Charleston and relating a conversation with a friend who had "lost his religion" because of the outcome of the war.

> *Dear Miss Sallie:*
>
> *…I was unable to leave Camden as early as I anticipated. Not that the place was so peculiarly fascinating, but Jimmy Wilson came over and spent ten days with us, and that occasioned a visit to Columbia. Such a sight I have never seen. A town of chimneys—nothing else standing. It more than*

realized all that I had ever read of desolation. Turning my back on so much desolation I started on my travels for this "burg" and managed to arrive safely. But what a change it presents. Nothing is as it was.

The negroes, the dirty, the very dirtiest class of country negroes are living in some of the best houses in our end of the town. Some of the old ones are glad to see those whom they formerly knew, and were as polite and respectful as ever, but the newly arrived are as saucy and impudent as can be, invariably take the inside of the pavement, and revel in every way in their newly acquired freedom. They seem to think it worthless unless they can make it offensive.

I found our house fortunately, in the possession of the wife of somebody in the [U.S.] Quartermaster's Department, a Mrs. Moses. She occupies the lower story, and promises to yield me the possession in a month as she intends leaving the City. I did the agreeable—complimented her on the good condition in which the premises were, and after exerting myself to make an impression, delicately suggested that if it were perfectly agreeable to her, and would not in any way inconvenience her, I would occupy upstairs. She, in turn did the agreeable, and assured me of the great satisfaction it would give her if I would move in.

So I hustled about and got a little furniture—a very little, and am now camped in the Drawing Room upstairs. A large unpainted pine table, on which I have the pleasure of writing you at the moment, is the central ornament, four crooked legged, broken back chairs, a gorgeous marble topped wash stand, and a large basin and a huge broken lipped pitcher complete the ornaments....

I sally out from all this luxury at eight in the morning, take a modest cup of coffee at a restaurant, dine at the same establishment, and get back to my den at five, and read, write or smoke in perfect independence. There are only about six children downstairs, and they do raise an awful row now and then, but a man can't have all the comforts of life at once. It is lucky that I am by nature of a domestic turn, for the "law" prohibits all persons from being out after eight in the evening, so visiting is not among my amusements.

It requires a vast deal of philosophy to keep cool, there is so much to try the temper, to make the blood boil, until you feel the tingling at the extremity of your foot—very much as if you would like to kick somebody. A good old friend of mine, pious above most men, took me out to a quiet spot and gravely imparted to me that he had lost his religion since the evacuation of the City. I looked my amazement, and he added, "I do want to curse, and I am afraid I curse internally." I advised him to go a secluded nook and air his propensity a little, and maybe he would feel more easy and be in a better frame of mind, and I should not be at all surprised to hear that he has been perverting his organ of speech. Even the ladies use words which a few years ago they would have pronounced too strong.…

Uncle William's house next door, is inhabited by soldiers and has been shockingly abused. They sing, dance and make night hideous. I rarely go to the window but what I see the blackest and dirtiest American citizens of African descent lolling from the windows, or dancing in the rooms, and nothing can be done to remedy it. The Military are all powerful. We can only bide our time and wait for the day of redemption. It must come shortly.

I do not believe it is the policy, for it is not the interest of the Government to ruin this section and make it as valueless to them as it is to us, and unless there is a change, nothing but ruin, utter, inevitable ruin can follow. They must soon see that they cannot regulate the vast emancipated problem.

Conner's mother, Juliana Conner, left Camden in late December 1865 and came to live with her son at their Meeting Street house, discovering to her dismay that, like many residences in Charleston, it had been pillaged.

Following the war, the Reverend Thomas Smyth, pastor of Second Presbyterian Church, returned to Charleston, where he found his home on Meeting Street "in a sad state." Soon after the Confederate evacuation, a surgeon in the Northern army took up residence in the Smyth home and lived there for months, selling all the furniture he could before he departed.[52]

The following excerpts are from letters written by Henry William DeSaussure Jr. to his father, Dr. Henry William DeSaussure. Henry was in Charleston, and his father was elsewhere but apparently wished to return to the city. On June 12, 1865, Henry reported:

My dear and honoured Father,

…I can only reiterate my advice to you to remain where you are. The city is filled up with negro troops insolent & overbearing; it requires great patience & self-control to be able to get along. They are no longer permitted to enter houses without a special order, nor openly to insult any one in the streets, but they do so, when they think they can without detection.…There is now I believe no molestation to refugees traveling through the country, and there will be no restriction imposed upon you in the city. But you will be obliged to take the oath of allegiance, or you will not be recognized as a citizen, or considered to have any rights at all. Gov. Aiken was <u>arrested</u> by a special

The home of William Aiken on Elizabeth Street in Charleston. *Library of Congress.*

messenger from Washington, at 9 o'clock at night, given ten minutes to get his clothes & take care of his wife but not allowed to be out of sight of the officer. [He was] carried at once to the provost marshal's office where he slept on the floor.

A couple of weeks later, on June 29, Henry W. DeSaussure wrote to his father:

The state of the city is melancholy enough.... The iron heel of despotism is upon us, and we are daily made to feel its weight. If this people had ever pictured to themselves what subjugation really meant, they never would have given up the contest while an army was left to wield a sword. But they vainly imagined that by yielding the contest, they would soon be restored to all their old political & personal rights. Filled with this mistaken notion, tired of a contest...they yielded and now they & their children must pay the bitter penalty. I have sent you some [newspapers]...which will convey to you better than I can the animus of the Northern people toward us. They are determined to make us drink to the dregs the cup of mortification & humiliation. Our country is ruined. The African labour will never cultivate it, white labour never can, the climate forbids.... We of the South are now destined to poverty, privation, & suffering.

The War in Berkeley County

Frederick A. Porcher's Account

Frederick Adolphus Porcher (1809–1888) was a historian and a professor at the College of Charleston. Formerly, he had been a planter in St. John's Berkeley Parish, in part of what is now Berkeley County, South Carolina, and he knew the whole region and its people well. About three years after the end of the war, Porcher wrote about what happened in his native parish and neighboring areas, recounting the depredations carried out by troops under the command of General Edward E. Potter and General Alfred S. Hartwell of the U.S. Army. The following is a portion of an untitled essay found among his papers.

> I have yet a painful task to perform before I conclude. I have to show how the people of this district were made to suffer by those agents of the radical power who vainly tried by every hellish device to involve the whole white population of the South in one indiscriminate massacre.[53]
>
> The hatred evinced by a large portion of the Northern people against the South can be explained only on one principle. They excelled us in wealth, population, in power; but they hated us all the more. They felt that in the great moral power of truthfulness and devotion to principle we were their superiors—hence they hated us. They forced us into war; they trusted that by means of their great resources we would be quickly crushed, but they found themselves baffled. All the honors of the war were ours; and when

they had worn out our strength they hated us the more because they were conscious that they owed their fortune to numbers alone; that the glory of the war would descend as an inheritance to the posterity of those who had fallen, and that in that posterity would again spring up and flourish that moral excellence which had always rebuked their groveling spirit. They earnestly decided to see that posterity crushed, extinguished. They desired the memory of Southern honor to disappear from the face of the earth.

The war came to an end too soon for the accomplishment of their benevolent purposes. To act the part of executioners except on the battlefield and by the slow torture of military prisons was too strong a measure for them to venture upon openly; they hoped to affect their object by means of the Negro.

Hence not content with the emancipation [of] the slave, he was diligently taught to regard himself as the equal, as the superior of his master. Arms were put in to his hands whilst they were taken from the whites; harangues were daily made to them to spur them on to acts of manhood. Gen. Saxton and Gen. Hatch[54] were constantly instructing them to assert their rights; and even Chief Justice Chase came from Washington to urge the Negro to triumph over his fallen master.[55] Whilst such speeches were daily spoken in Charleston to eager and admiring throngs of Negroes, there was not an armed white man in the District of Charleston. There was not a citizen of either sex who entertained even a wish to oppose the emancipation of slavery, the issue of the war.

The last division of the Confederate Army had crossed Goose Creek on the 20th February and destroyed the bridge. The Army of the United States was at the time in Charleston. Their commanders knew how poorly provided the retreating army was, and might easily have overtaken them. But they made no attempt to do so. They had nobler game in view. What that game was and how they pursued it let the following extracts from the letter of a lady[56] show. The household she described consisted of five ladies, one of who was weighed down with the burden of nearly four score years.

[She wrote:] On the afternoon of Feb. 22nd, as we were preparing to take our usual walk, troops were seen coming up the avenue whom we recognized by their blue dress to be U.S. soldiers. All five of us stood in the piazza to receive them, and if possible

General John P. Hatch (1822–1901) was the military commander of Charleston District from February to August 1865. *Library of Congress.*

prevent their entrance. The first come, Lieut. R., smirked, sneered and jeered. His first question was: "Where's the man of the house?" We answered: "He is not here." "In the rebel army, I suppose?" No answer. Then turning to his men he said: "This woman here (pointing to mamma) says that old lady (maum Martha) can get you some poultry." He then said: "I suppose you have never seen black troops. You will soon have the pleasure as they are coming up now." Mamma answered: "I am accustomed to Negroes, and never have feared them. Negroes have always behaved well to me."

We now saw coming up the avenue the rudest looking savages I ever beheld. They came shouting, pointing their guns and making horrid grimaces. A little white officer, Lieut. J., headed them, who seemed fiercely excited. He screamed to mamma: "I have come Madam to liberate your people." Mamma replied: "I hope you will be kind to them. They are accustomed to kindness." This seemed to infuriate the little man who shrieked: "That is a strange thing for a southern woman to say to an officer of black troops." He then turned to his black savages and said: "Boys, take what you can find." In an instant, the barns, storerooms, smoke house and dairy were broken open and emptied, and the cattle, sheep, hogs, mules, horses and poultry driven off. Mamma said to Lieut. J, who was looking calmly at this work of destruction: "If you deprive us of all means of subsistence, we must starve." He said: "You are now suffering for what you have done." Then turning to the house servants who had gathered around us he called Quash, saying: "Uncle, follow me." "Yes, Maussa," said Quash, at which the little man exclaimed: "For God's sake, don't call me master." Then calling to the maids he said: "That woman (meaning mamma) is a very wicked woman. I know she has hid things. You must show me where they are. The rebel man has gone to the wars, but he has left a d----d rebel of a woman, and I want her head." The maids said they knew of nothing concealed, and that Missus was not wicked. This he refused to believe and insisted on going upstairs by the back way. He searched about, and going into our dressing room where Fanny's bed lay on the floor, he walked to A.'s large trunk saying: "I will open this." Fanny adroitly said: "Oh sir, this is my room and everything in it is mine." He said: "Oh, Madam, when you go to town you shall have a better room, but nothing of yours will I touch." He then opened my writing desk, which lay on the table, saying: "But Madam, this is not yours." Fanny was afraid to claim too much; so he looked over my papers and put a handful of letters in his pocket. Then strutting into the sleeping room he wished to search the presses and drawers. Fanny said: "You will find nothing but my young ladies clothes. Please don't trouble them." He said: "Madam, you seem much interested in your young ladies; you are a great fool for it they are the worst friends you can have!"

Meanwhile a crowd surrounded the house and filled the lawn. Blacks and whites together came rushing up with pointed bayonets, evidently intent upon entering the house. A. stepped up to a man who seemed to look disapprovingly upon the scene, and said: "I look to you for protection." He said: "They shall not enter," and stood in the doorway. By this time it was dark, and the confusion outside increasing, we closed the doors, and sat, expecting at every moment to be invaded. At last the door was burst open, and several tall military figures entered. They surveyed the apartment without taking any notice of us. One of them taking up a candle opened the door of mamma's room and said: "This is a nice room, General, You will do well to remain here." The general nodded assent, and mamma then advanced and said: "Gen. Potter, I presume?" He nodded. She continued: "I have always been in the habit of extending hospitality to those who come to my house; but as I see by your manner that you come as a master, I suppose it is needless to ask you to be seated." He threw himself into a chair, and after surveying the room and its occupants, he and his aids made some efforts at conversation, which were sustained by aunt C. who was made affable by extreme terror. We all slept upstairs, leaving the lower story to the general and his suite. In the morning when he was going mamma asked him for a protection, as we would be in constant danger from the number of camps in the neighborhood. His reply was: "Madam, your husband is in the rebel army." Mamma said: "I am glad he is not here; some violence would certainly have been offered him last evening." The general turned and said with great politeness: "Madam, you talk like a fool." And he would have left us at the mercy of his brutal soldiers had not one of his aids, who carried a heart beneath his blue coat, insisted on writing a protection paper in the general's name. It was of great use to us afterwards.

This extract shows clearly the animus with which Gen. Potter left Charleston. The retreating army was just ahead of him, but his object was not to expose his precious life to the hazard of a battle. His noble mission was to insult and outrage defenseless women to excite the dormant passions of the Negroes and make them the instrument of exterminating the hated Southern race. He takes possession of a lady's bedchamber without even an apology, and when she begs him for a protection against the barbarians who had so cruelly outraged her household, he replies: "Your husband is in the rebel army!" This lady and her family had remained at their home in trustful reliance upon that law of manhood universally recognized that soldiers never outrage the defenseless. But this man had no manhood. His mission was to outrage the defenseless. Had he hastened the march of his troops he might have found men. It was more congenial to his disposition to insult women.

Five days afterwards a part of this general's command entered Pineville. With that proclivity to outrage every thing that is venerable, they had called at Pooshee and amused themselves by pelting the venerable Dr. Ravenel in his own house, with some eggs that lay upon the sideboard.[57] This was their amusement. But they did not neglect their business, which was to rob his house of silver and other valuables. As soon as this band of brigands entered Pineville, they exhibited their dexterity in opening closets and storerooms, and helping themselves to whatsoever they could find. But this was not enough. Three days afterwards the noble general arrived with a force of two thousand men and they completed the spoliation which had been commenced by their vanguard, and this heartless robbery of defenseless women was carried on whilst the general was in the very house that was the object of plunder. He remained in Pineville but a few hours.

South Carolina in 1865

Pooshee Plantation house, the home of Dr. Henry William Ravenel, as it appeared in the early twentieth century. *Library of Congress.*

Perhaps he had a spark of shame still lurking about him and was unwilling to witness what he was determined to perform. The next day a major and a captain with a few followers entered the devoted village and began to fire the houses.[58] Dr. Rene Ravenel,[59] who was there, remonstrated against this wanton destruction of property, showing how these houses were the retreats of the people from the pestiferous atmosphere, which in summer surrounds the adjacent country. This information only whetted their thirst for destruction, inasmuch as they could now gratify their cruelty at the same time that they exercised their vandalism. One house they said is enough for a rebel, and the torch was applied to a dozen. Col. James Ferguson, an old blind man eighty-five years of age, occupied one of these. But he had committed inexpiable crimes. He was a gentleman, and he was the father of Gen. Ferguson. He and his wife and daughters were mercilessly turned out and his house fired. The courage and devotion of one Negro man saved the house of his mistress, and the Episcopal Church, which was twice fired.

After these acts of vandalism, Gen. Potter retired with his laurels to the neighbourhood of Charleston. Arms and ammunition had been freely distributed among the Negroes, and no pains spared to urge them to complete the work which he had only commenced, and which a dread of public opinion prevented him from completing. His commander Gen. Hatch not only approved this, but also declared to Mr. W. Mazyck Porcher that had he commanded the expedition he would have given arms to more Negroes than Gen. Potter had done.[60] Against whom were these arms to be used? There was not at that time a Confederate soldier within the limits of Charleston District. There was scarcely a man capable of bearing arms.[61]

Gen. Ferguson, whose brigade was waiting orders in Newberry, having heard of the ruthless manner in which the brigands, now joined by many of the Negroes, were harassing the people, sent a detachment of his troops to scour the country, protect the citizens, and repress the insolence of these lawless people.[62] As long as they remained hereabouts the brigands were quelled, and order restored. On one occasion a body of these troops, having been fired upon by a large gang of armed Negroes, a fight took place near Pineville, and the Negroes were dispersed with the loss

Left: General Samuel Wragg Ferguson (1834–1917). His elderly father, James Ferguson, left his vandalized plantation, Dockon, to take refuge in Pineville. *Wikimedia Commons*.

Right: General Alfred S. Hartwell (1836–1912) in 1858. *Wikimedia Commons*.

of about twenty of their number. Gen. Ferguson's orders having caused him to move his position, his scouts were recalled, and then the valiant Gen. Hartwell appeared upon the scene.

His avowed object was to "avenge the murder of the Negroes by guerillas," the same Negroes who had commenced the work of death with the arms, which his own people had put in their hands. His plan of revenge was characteristic. He proposed to destroy the few houses, which Potter had left in Pineville, houses occupied by women and children. On his way to Pineville he stopped at Woodlawn, the residence of Mr. Wm. F. Ravenel, who had been compelled by illness to leave the army.[63] Hartwell arrested him and took him from his house. Dr. Morton Waring, who was there at the time, remonstrated against the cruelty, assuring the general that Mr. Ravenel's life would be put in peril by his removal. His remonstrance was so far effectual that the sick man was put into a wagon instead of being made to follow his captor on foot, whilst one of his aids helped himself to his best horse. Mr. Ravenel was detained in custody several days without knowing his crime, and after being dragged about as long as it pleased his tyrant, he was dismissed at Eutaw and allow[ed] finding his way home as best he could.

Gen. Hartwell, having learned to his satisfaction that the Negroes, who had been dispersed by Ferguson's scouts, had not been murdered by the old ladies of Pineville, magnanimously abandoned his purpose of revenge, and sought some more worthy object upon which to exercise his valor. A Negro pointed out the desired object. The security of the Negroes and the good of the country depended upon the removal of Mr. William Mazyck Porcher. To accomplish this great object, he started for Mr. Porcher's plantation with a force of upwards of a thousand soldiers.

Mr. Porcher, a gentleman beyond the military age, was living at home, trusting to the strength of Gen. Sherman's promise of protection to person and property to all who remained quietly at home.[64] He might have trusted to the established usage of civilized nations, of which Sherman's promise was only ratification. His home was his paternal inheritance, had been his father's homestead and was endeared to him by the recollections and associations of a lifetime. This was precisely the sort of home that seemed to stir up the worst feelings of these malignant wretches. Mr. Porcher had suffered robbery at the hands of Potter's brigands. This was soon to be forgotten under the atrocity sanctioned by the enlightened Hartwell. Having halted his force at a short distance from the house, his Adjutant General, accompanied by a private guard, galloped up to the dwelling and captured Mr. Porcher. This important work achieved, the general came up mounted on a horse, which he had found in a neighbouring stable. He entered the piazza, seated himself and called his prisoner to him. At the moment the latter saw the soldiers taking away some silverware and other valuables, which had been committed to him for safekeeping. Mindful of his trust, he thought his captor might also respect it, and he said to him: "General, respect that property, it is not mine; it belongs to a friend." To this he replied imperiously: "Ask no favors, sir; none shall be granted you. I have information against you of a very serious nature, and if you escape with your life, you will have much to be grateful for." To the inquiry what was his crime, he said: "That will be laid before the Provost Marshall of Charleston, before whom you must appear. Not a word more from you, sir." The night was spent there, and the next morning all the plantation building[s] which contained cotton, corn, looms, every building, which on inquiry they had ascertained to be valuable, was fired and destroyed in Hartwell's presence. Before leaving the house that morning the drawers and closets were opened and everything of value was taken out, such as silver and plated ware, jewelry, towels, napkins, etc. All his clothing was stolen except a change in a carpetbag, which had been secreted in her house by a faithful servant, and the general started with his prisoner. Two of his aids remained behind to finish the work of destruction. In pursuance of orders they burnt the dwelling house. So said Cap. [Brown] his adjutant.

I have already noticed their doings at Mr. James Gaillard's plantation.[65] At Walworth, the residence of Mr. Thomas W. Porcher, they called for wine. Mrs. Porcher declared there was none in the house but some miserable blackberry wine. It was given to them, and not liking the taste, they compelled her to drink some of it, fearing lest it might have been drugged. They stole all the silver, and went off with their horses laden with quilts, blankets, curtains, etc. They took whatever struck their fancy. A gentleman, who travelled over the state road soon after Hartwell's raid, informed me that the road was strewn with feathers, which had been wantonly taken out of the numerous pillows, bolsters and beds, which these marauders had plundered during their visit to St. John's.

Wherever these wretches went the same exhibition was made, of fiendish hatred of everything that was venerable, of wanton disregard of private property, of insolent bearing towards innocence and helplessness. At the family residence of the Middletons in St. Andrew's Parish, the house was rifled of old and valuable pictures and the family cemetery violated.

Where acts of violence, of rapine and of plunder follow the taking of a town by storm, though the exhibition is horrible, we make some allowances for the excitement, which follows a battle. In a few hours the excitement wears away and the soldiers are ashamed of their excesses. There were no such exciting causes here. These armies had not escaped the perils of battle. The country had been abandoned to their mercy, and their acts of violence and plunder were deliberately performed.

When Mr. Porcher was taken before the Provost Marshall in Charleston, no charge was brought against him. He was detained on parole several days in order that his captor might have time to invent one; but none was ever made. So his silver and other valuables were kept...and he was discharged.

Gen. Hartwell was rather sore at the publication in a New York paper of his doings near Pineville, and prevailed with two Carolinians to endeavor to whitewash him. This they did very lamely. In fact they could not without convicting Mr. Porcher of falsehood, clear their protégé of the charge of being an incendiary, a ruffian, and something very nearly resembling a thief.

The Confederate States were either an independent state fighting a defensive war, or her people were rebels. If the former, Mr. Porcher's person was sacred, and nothing short of military necessity could justify the seizure or the destruction of his property. If they were rebels (and this is the light in which the people of the U.S. regard them), then as the minister of the law Gen. Hartwell might arrest Mr. Porcher as a rebel, and deliver him to the proper tribunals for trial. But the moment the arrest was made the property of the accused was a sacred trust in his hands, to be kept inviolate until the law had pronounced its judgment upon the prisoner. Any opposition to his will did not justify the exhibition of violence. The prisoner submitted, and every principle of justice was violated. The capture was made, the property destroyed, the movables appropriated; and to show how completely this was the act of a ruffian, after he had seized, humbled and insulted his prisoner, burned his house and stolen his property, he took him to Charleston and then dismissed him.[66]

Epilogue

Just before the first day of the year 1865, Joseph LeConte, a former professor at South Carolina College, was in Georgia trying to find his daughter Sallie and bring her back to their home in Columbia. Sherman's army had completed its destructive march across Georgia, and what LeConte saw and heard there filled him with despair—and with dread that the South would lose the war and its bid for independence. In a journal he kept, he lamented:

> *In my daily solitary walks I have wrestled in agony with this demon of despair. My anxiety for the safety of my friends and of my daughter, the certain loss of everything I own as property—all, all is swallowed up in the dread of this one great all-including calamity. For four long years the whole heart of the nation has beat for this Cause alone. For this sons, brothers, husbands, fathers have been freely sacrificed; for this earnest agonizing prayers have gone up daily from every church and every family circle. O God! and must it fail at last!*[67]

In February 1865, less than a week after Columbia's burning, LeConte and his daughter returned to the city, and he recorded his first impressions in his journal:

> *We entered Columbia at the extreme northern end (Cottontown) and went down the whole length of Main Street for a mile and a half. Not a house*

remaining. Only the tall chimneys standing gaunt and spectral, and empty brick walls with vacant windows like death-heads with eyeless sockets. The fire had swept five or six blocks wide right through the heart of the city. Only the eastern and western outskirts are left. We met not a living soul—"Alas, how the beautiful city, the Pride of the State, sits desolate and in ashes!"[68]

LeConte's fears were fulfilled when the war ended in Southern defeat a few months later.

Like Columbia, much of Charleston lay in ruins. Sidney Andrews, a Northern visitor who arrived in the city just after the war, observed:

A city of ruins, of desolation, of vacant houses, of widowed women, of rotting wharves, of deserted warehouses, of weed-wild gardens, of miles of grass grown streets, of acres of pitiful and voiceful barrenness—this Charleston.... The beauty and pride of the city are as dead as the glories of Athens.... Now one marks how few young men there are, how generally the young women are dressed in black. The flower of their proud aristocracy is buried on scores of battle-fields.

William L. Trenholm of Charleston looked back on these days, recalling that the city "lay like a wreck on the shore; the region around her was desolate and barren, every prospect was dismal, every circumstance strange to all past experiences." And as bad as things were in Charleston, he wrote, "the surrounding country was literally an unproductive waste." Trenholm elaborated:

The rice plantations had been generally abandoned and had consequently relapsed into swamps; the labor had been removed from them and in many cases the buildings and machinery had been destroyed. The sea islands had early fallen within the military lines on one side or the other, the property in the lands over a large area had passed away from the owners, the labor was utterly demoralized and considered irreclaimable.

Every railroad leading out of Charleston had lost bridges and trestles, on some the track had been torn up for miles, none had adequate equipment for even the limited business offering, nor were the means at once obtainable for renewing the worn out rails and cross-ties.

Writing of the Lowcountry plantation lands surrounding Charleston, historian Samuel Gaillard Stoney observed that many plantation houses, "in

Epilogue

Cedar Spring, a Porcher family plantation in Berkeley County, as it appeared in the early twentieth century. *Library of Congress.*

the grim poverty and wholesale demoralization" after the war, "were simply abandoned to perish by slow dilapidation or burn in forest fires." Some rice plantations were revived for a while, but in the early part of the twentieth century, they too were mostly abandoned. "For the better part of the decade that followed the [first] World War," Stoney added, "the Low Country was a region of deserted fields growing up in a forest, of ragged dying gardens and grim, cold, pathetic houses, solemnly awaiting their doom."[69]

After the war and the ordeal of the Reconstruction years that followed it, economic recovery in South Carolina took many decades. E. Milby Burton, who wrote a history of Charleston during the war, asserted that in 1865, "Charleston was as good as dead." But he ended his wartime chronicle on a hopeful note:

> *No federal aid to rebuild the great city was to be expected, and for a long time none came. There was only one reason for hope: the city's location. At the tip of the peninsula where, as Charlestonians say, "the Ashley and the Cooper meet and form the Atlantic Ocean," the city was and still is the natural port for a large area of the South and Midwest. Very slowly, commerce was revived.*

Epilogue

And the city's poverty eventually became her greatest blessing. In the early twentieth century, Charlestonians could not afford to pull down their old buildings and put up new ones. As a result, when World War II finally brought prosperity again, those buildings that had survived the holocaust of the Civil War were refurbished and still stand today.

Notes

Introduction

1. Reid, *Ohio in the War*, 475.
2. Taylor, *Leverett Letters*, 388.

Part I

3. Isabella Middleton Cheves (1826–1912), the widow of Dr. Charles Manly Cheves and one of the daughters of Henry A. Middleton.
4. Ella was Eleanor Maria Middleton Rutledge (1831–1905), the wife of Benjamin Huger Rutledge Jr.
5. This was Oliver Hering Middleton, who was close to seventy years old. His young son Oliver was killed in battle in 1864.
6. Hal was Harriott Horry Rutledge Ravenel (Mrs. St. Julien Ravenel).
7. This was Anna Raven Vanderhorst Lewis (1830–1865), wife of John Williams Lewis. She died on February 26, 1865. In her famous diary, Mary Boykin Chesnut wrote, "Dr. Miles told us that Mrs. Lewis, nee Vanderhorst, died of fright during the Columbia fire." Chesnut, *Diary from Dixie*, 506.
8. Langdon Cheves (1848–1939) was the teenage son of Isabella Middleton Cheves. He left Columbia to join his regiment in Virginia.
9. Alice Middleton, one of Henry A. Middleton's daughters.
10. Julia Emma Rhett Middleton (1835–1908), wife of Arthur Middleton.
11. Eweretta Elizabeth Middleton (1840–1899), the widow of Thomas Middleton (1832–1864). Lizzie was Elizabeth Middleton Smith (Mrs. John Julius Pringle Smith).
12. Lise and Sally were nieces of Harriott Horry Rutledge Ravenel.

Part II

13. Mrs. Wallace was likely Sallie Davie Burroughs Wallace (1837–1917), the wife of Dr. Alfred Wallace (1835–1890). She had a son named Alfred who was born on November 23, 1863.
14. Reprinted courtesy of the *Confederate Veteran* magazine.
15. General Halleck's suggestion to General Sherman (*War of the Rebellion, Official Records of the Union and Confederate Armies* [hereafter *War of the Rebellion*], series 1, vol. 44) that "should you capture Charleston I hope that by *some accident* the place may be destroyed, and should a little salt be sown upon its site, it may prevent the growth of future crops of nullification and secession," was met with ready approval. "I will bear in mind your hint as to Charleston, and don't think salt will be necessary," said General Sherman in reply. "When I move the Fifteenth Corps will be on the right of the right wing, and their position will naturally bring them into Charleston first, and if you have studied the history of that corps you will have remarked that they generally do up their work pretty well." The army, as we shall see, changed its course and did not enter Charleston but selected, instead, Columbia. The efficient Fifteenth Corps mentioned in Sherman's letter to Halleck was the principal unit trusted with its occupation.
16. *War of the Rebellion*, series 1, vol. 47. Sherman neglects to mention in the report that he burned Orangeburg while there.
17. A beautiful new state capitol building was still under construction in Columbia.
18. Sherman's army numbered over sixty thousand.
19. "In his oft-cited book *Sherman and the Burning of Columbia*, Marion Brunson Lucas blames Sherman for not taking enough action to prevent the inferno and Hampton for not taking enough steps to prevent the cotton from being set afire....However, several witnesses Lucas did not cite in his book state that there was no cotton burning when the Confederates left." Elmore, *Carnival of Destruction*, 268. Tom Elmore, who spent over a decade and a half researching Sherman's South Carolina campaign, contended that most of the evidence puts the primary blame for the burning of the city on Sherman's troops. In her recent book *Sherman's Flame and Blame Campaign*, Patricia McNeely stated that the evidence that Sherman's men destroyed Columbia was overwhelming.
20. The *Daily Record* (Columbia, SC), July 22, 1911; Wade Hampton, letter in *Baltimore Enquirer*, June 24, 1873; Gen. M.C. Butler Affidavit of August 20, 1866.

Notes to Pages 57–86

21. The cause of the war.
22. Lieutenant John A. McQueen of the Fifteenth Illinois Cavalry.
23. General Preston had befriended the Catholics in Columbia before the war, encouraging the opening of the convent school, which had been opposed by some. Sherman actually executed titles to the house and property, deeding it to the convent in return for the house his men had destroyed. The nuns used the Preston house as a convent until after the war, when the Mother Superior restored it to General Preston, thus discharging the obligation she owed the family.
24. Sherman, *Memoirs*, 288.
25. *War of the Rebellion*, series 1, vol. 47, part 1, 22.
26. *War of the Rebellion*, series 1, vol. 44, 810.
27. *War of the Rebellion*, series 1, vol. 47, part 3, 351.
28. *War of the Rebellion*, series 1, vol. 47, part 1, 170.
29. *War of the Rebellion*, series 1, vol. 47, part 1, 227.
30. *War of the Rebellion*, series 1, vol. 47, part 1, 252.
31. *War of the Rebellion*, series 1, vol. 47, part 1, 272.
32. *War of the Rebellion*, series 1, vol. 47, part 1, 457.
33. General Howard also lied to Mrs. Louisa S. McCord, whose house he used as his headquarters in Columbia.
34. Testimony heard before Mixed Commission on British and American Claims, Washington, D.C., 1873.
35. *War of the Rebellion*, series 3, vol. 5, 406.
36. The gentlemen constituting this committee were all citizens of the highest standing in the community, both social and professional. Professor John LeConte was a man of international reputation in the realms of science and education. He afterward became organizer and first executive head of the University of California, where both he and his remarkable brother, Joseph LeConte, the geologist, completed their brilliant careers.
37. *War of the Rebellion*, series 1, vol. 47, part 1, 309.
38. This was Dr. Daniel H. Trezevant.
39. She means General John A. Logan, commander of the Fifteenth Corps.
40. In a letter to her son dated February 24, 1865, Mary Maxcy Leverett wrote of what she had been told about the conduct of the Union soldiers outside the asylum: "The fiends raged cursing, screaming up and down in front of the Asylum swearing they were going to blow up the Asylum that night." Taylor, *Leverett Letters*, 386.
41. Mary Maxcy Leverett wrote of this in a letter: "One lady had a baby only a few minutes old she was very ill and Dr. Trezevant who was with

her, saw the Yankee soldiers take matches & deliberately set fire to the house she was in, three times & each time some more humane, put it out, and even prepared a litter to carry her out in case the others succeeded." Taylor, *Leverett Letters*, 386–87.
42. Beginning in March 1865, in the first ten issues of a newspaper called the *Columbia Phoenix*, renowned author William Gilmore Simms published a series of powerful eyewitness accounts of the burning of Columbia. In 2005, those issues were published as *A City Laid Waste*, edited by David Aiken.

Part III

43. *War of the Rebellion*, series 1, vol. 47, part 2, 641.
44. Cardozo, *Reminiscences of Charleston*, 76–78.
45. Burton, *Siege of Charleston*, 323.
46. Holmes, *Historic Sketch*, 28.
47. Williams, *St. Michael's*, 99.
48. Irby, "After Civil War."
49. Powers, *Black Charlestonians*, 78.
50. The worst outbreak of smallpox in South Carolina occurred in 1865, with a death toll of about thirty thousand. A resident of James Island (near Charleston) reported that in the summer and fall of 1865, "500 negroes" died of smallpox in a plantation house being used as a hospital. Stokes, *Incidents in the Life*, 77.
51. Fraser, *Charleston! Charleston!*, 274.
52. Smyth, *Autobiographical Notes*, 675.
53. In July 1862, Porcher wrote to his wife: "Appearances in the Yankee army indicate that the war is rapidly becoming on their side a war of extermination. In fact the Herald indicates that after the war there will be splendid fields in Tennessee and elsewhere inviting emigrants from Europe. These fields can become vacant only through the extermination of the present occupants." On May 24, 1861, an editorial in the *Daily Herald*, a newspaper of Newburyport, Massachusetts, stated, "If it were necessary, we could clear off the thousand millions of square miles [of the South] so that not a city or cultivated field would remain; we could exterminate nine millions of white people and re-settle—re-people the lands."
54. Rufus Saxton and John P. Hatch were Union generals headquartered in Charleston.

55. When U.S. Chief Justice Salmon P. Chase visited Charleston in May 1865, he made a speech before the newly freed people of the city.
56. Frederick A. Porcher's cousin Marion Johnstone Porcher, writing about events at Otranto (or Goslington) Plantation near Charleston.
57. Dr. Henry Ravenel (1798–1867) was one of the largest planters in Middle St. John's Parish.
58. In her 1865 diary, Susan R. Jervey, a resident of St. John's Parish, wrote of Pineville: "It seems completely given up to the negroes. They have burnt all unoccupied houses. The freed negroes from the neighbouring plantations seem worse than the Yankees, are destroying and burning everything around the village." Jervey, *Two Diaries*, 11.
59. Dr. René Ravenel (1826–1875) of Pooshee Plantation, the son of Dr. Henry Ravenel.
60. William Mazyck Porcher (1812–1902) of Mexico Plantation in St. Stephen's Parish.
61. Porcher's niece Marion Porcher wrote from Charleston on June 11, 1865, that the "Yankees" were trying to stir up racial animosity, commenting, "Everything is done to infuriate the negroes against the whites."
62. In General Samuel Wragg Ferguson's journal of March 19, 1865, he recorded that he had dispatched "Lieutenant Pettus with scout to watch the enemy about Pineville and Charleston." Sloan, *Samuel Wragg Ferguson*, 19.
63. William Francis Ravenel (1828–1896), the son of Dr. Henry Ravenel of Pooshee.
64. General Sherman's orders about the destruction of civilian property in South Carolina were seldom obeyed by his soldiers. "On paper only unoccupied houses were allowed to be destroyed, but these orders were often violated." One of his officers, General Alpheus S. Williams, observed: "Orders to respect houses and private property not necessary for subsistence of the army were not greatly heeded. Indeed, not heeded at all." Elmore, *Carnival of Destruction*, 90, 92.
65. In another memoir, Frederick A. Porcher had previously written about the "doings" at Walnut Grove, James Gaillard's plantation, remarking: "Mr. Gaillard is at this time the oldest and most respected inhabitant of this country.…But neither his character nor his age could save him from the brutality of Gen. A.S. Hartwell.…Mr. Gaillard's house was plundered, and personal indignities were offered to him by Adjutant Gen. Torrey, the aid of Hartwell." Porcher, "Upper Beat of St. John's Berkeley," 60.

66. After William Mazyck Porcher was taken from his plantation, called Mexico, his house was looted and burned by U.S. soldiers. He was never charged with any crime.

Epilogue

67. LeConte, *'Ware Sherman*, 23.
68. Ibid., 140.
69. Stoney, *Plantations of the Carolina Low Country*, 42.

Bibliography

Alden, Henry Mills. "Four Years Under Fire at Charleston." *Harper's New Monthly Magazine*, June–November 1865.

Andrews, Sidney. *The South Since the War.* New York: Arno Press, 1969.

Burton, E. Milby. *The Siege of Charleston, 1861–1865.* Columbia: University of South Carolina Press, 1970.

Cardozo, Jacob N. *Reminiscences of Charleston.* Charleston, SC: Joseph Walker, 1866.

Carroll, James Parsons. *Report of the Committee Appointed to Collect Testimony in Relation to the Destruction of Columbia, S.C., on the 17th of February, 1865.* Columbia, SC: Bryan Printing Company, 1893.

Chesnut, Mary Boykin. *A Diary from Dixie.* Edited by Ben Ames Williams. Cambridge, MA: Harvard University Press, 1980.

Conrad, August. *The Destruction of Columbia, S.C., A Translation of the German by Wm. H. Pleasants.* Roanoke, VA: Stone Printing and Manufacturing Company, 1902.

Cote, Richard N. *Mary's World.* Mt. Pleasant, SC: Corinthian Books, 2001.

Edgar, Walter B. "Sesquicentennial Address." *South Carolina Historical Magazine*, April–July 2005.

Elmore, Tom. *A Carnival of Destruction: Sherman's Invasion of South Carolina.* Charleston, SC: Joggling Board Press, 2012.

Fraser, Walter J. *Charleston! Charleston! The History of a Southern City.* Columbia: University of South Carolina Press, 1989.

French, J. Clement. *The Trip of the Steamer Oceanus to Fort Sumter and Charleston, S.C.* Brooklyn, NY: Union Steam Printing House, 1865.

Bibliography

Holmes, George S. *A Historic Sketch of the Parish Church of St. Michael, in the Province of South Carolina.* Charleston, SC: Walker, Evans & Cogswell, 1887.

Huger, Alfred. "The Burning of Columbia: Letter from Hon. Alfred Huger." *New York World*, August 22, 1866.

Irby, Laurens H. "After Civil War: Rector Banned Over Prayer." *News & Courier*, December 28, 1964.

Irving, John Beaufain. *A Day on the Cooper River* (Enlarged and edited by Louisa Cheves Stoney; reprinted with notes by Samuel Gaillard Stoney). Columbia, SC: R.L. Bryan Company, 1969.

Jervey, Susan Ravenel. *Two Diaries From Middle St. John's, Berkeley, South Carolina, February–May, 1865.* Pinopolis, SC: St. John's Hunting Club, 1921.

LeConte, Joseph. *'Ware Sherman: A Journal of Three Months' Personal Experience in the Last Days of the Confederacy.* Baton Rouge: Louisiana State University Press, 1999.

Milling, Chapman J. "Ilium in Flames." *Confederate Veteran Magazine*, June 1928.

Porcher, Frederick A. "A Newly Discovered Chapter of Frederick A. Porcher's 'Upper Beat of St. John's Berkeley.'" *South Carolina Historical Magazine*, July 2016.

———. "Upper Beat of St. John's Berkeley: A Memoir." *Transactions of the Huguenot Society* 13 (1906): 31–78.

Powers, Bernard E. *Black Charlestonians: A Social History, 1822–1885.* Fayetteville: University of Arkansas Press, 1994.

Reid, Whitelaw. *Ohio in the War: Her Statesmen, Generals and Soldiers.* Columbus, OH: Eclectic Publishing Company, 1893.

Schurz, Carl. *The Reminiscences of Carl Schurz.* New York: McClure Company, 1908.

Scott, Edwin J. *Random Recollections of a Long Life, 1806 to 1876.* Columbia, SC: Charles A. Calvo, Jr., Publisher, 1884.

Sherman, William T. *Memoirs of Gen. W. T. Sherman.* New York: L. Webster, 1892.

Sloan, E.D. *Samuel Wragg Ferguson, 1834–1917: Brigadier General, C.S.A.: Memoirs and 1865 Journal.* Greenville, SC: E.D. Sloan Jr., 1998.

Smyth, Thomas. *Autobiographical Notes, Letters and Reflections.* Charleston, SC: Walker, Evans & Cogswell Co., 1914.

Stokes, Karen. *Incidents in the Life of Cecilia Lawton: A Memoir of Plantation Life, War, and Reconstruction in Georgia and South Carolina.* Macon, GA: Mercer University Press, 2021.

———. *South Carolina Civilians in Sherman's Path.* Charleston, SC: The History Press, 2012.

Stoney, Samuel Gaillard. *Plantations of the Carolina Low Country.* Charleston, SC: Carolina Art Association, 1938.

Taylor, Frances Wallace, ed. *The Leverett Letters: Correspondence of a South Carolina Family, 1851–1868.* Columbia: University of South Carolina Press, 2000.

Trenholm, William L. *The Centennial Address before the Charleston Chamber of Commerce, 11th February, 1884.* Charleston, SC: News & Courier Presses, 1884.

War of the Rebellion. The Official Records of the Union and Confederate Armies. Washington, D.C.: Government Printing Office, 1880–1909.

Williams, George W. *St. Michael's, Charleston, 1751–1951.* Columbia: University of South Carolina Press, 1951.

Manuscripts and Archival Resources

Bancroft Library, University of California, Berkeley:
LeConte, Josephine. Letter, February 28, 1865. LeConte Family Papers: additions, BANC MSS C-B 1014.
Hargrett Library, University of Georgia:
Cornelius C. Platter Civil War Diary, 1864–1865.
South Carolina Historical Society:
Caroline Howard Gilman Papers. South Carolina Historical Society (SCHS).
Conner Family Papers.
DeSaussure Family Papers.
Frederick A. Porcher Papers.
John B. Irving Legal Papers.
Lee, Eliza Lucilla Haskell. "Reminiscences of Troublous Times, and God's Special Providences."
Middleton, Harriott. Letter to Susan Middleton, February 28, 1865. Logan Family Papers.
William Black Yates Reminiscences.
South Caroliniana Library, University of South Carolina:
Grace Brown Elmore Diary, 1860–1866.

Other

Grundy, Charles. Letter, April 26, 1865. Lot #580, 2005-09. Raynor's Historical Collectible Auctions.

About the Author

Karen Stokes has been an archivist at the South Carolina Historical Society in Charleston for over twenty-five years. Her special area of interest is the Confederate period, and she has authored and edited numerous books and articles on the subject, including three History Press publications: *South Carolina Civilians in Sherman's Path* (2012), *The Immortal 600: Surviving Civil War Charleston and Savannah* (2013) and *Confederate South Carolina: True Stories of Civilians, Soldiers and the War* (2015). Her most recent scholarly books, published by Mercer University Press, are *An Everlasting Circle: Letters of the Haskell Family of Abbeville, South Carolina, 1861–1865* (2019) and *Incidents in the Life of Cecilia Lawton: A Memoir of Plantation Life, War, and Reconstruction in Georgia and South Carolina* (2021).